LEAVING HOME

More in the Classic Wisdom for Modern Minds
series from Macmillan Collector's Library

Falling in Love

Finding Happiness

Living Peacefully

LEAVING HOME

Selection and introduction by Zachary Seager

M

MACMILLAN COLLECTOR'S LIBRARY

This collection first published 2025 by Macmillan Collector's Library
an imprint of Pan Macmillan
The Smithson, 6 Briset Street, London EC1M 5NR
EU representative: Macmillan Publishers Ireland Ltd,
1st Floor, The Liffey Trust Centre, 117–126 Sheriff Street Upper,
Dublin 1, D01 YC43
Associated companies throughout the world
www.panmacmillan.com

ISBN 978-1-0350-4563-1

1 3 5 7 9 8 6 4 2

A CIP catalogue record for this book is available from the British Library.

Typeset in Plantin by Jouve (UK), Milton Keynes
Printed and bound in China by Imago

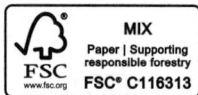

MIX
Paper | Supporting
responsible forestry
FSC
www.fsc.org
FSC® C116313

Visit **www.panmacmillan.com** to read more
about all our books and to buy them.

Contents

FINDING YOUR PATH

Introduction

All of literature can be divided into two basic narratives, said Leo Tolstoy. A person goes on a journey or a stranger comes to town.

Leaving aside the fact that the author of *War and Peace* almost certainly never made this claim, there would be no literature, no myth, no stories at all if Odysseus had never left Ithaca, if Don Quixote had decided to remain in his small village in La Mancha, if Alice had kept her balance at the edge of the rabbit hole, or if Dorothy had stayed in Kansas. Even the stranger in that apocryphal Tolstoy quotation had to leave home at some point to arrive in a new town. Every story worth telling starts in earnest with leaving home.

That doesn't make it any easier. Leaving home is at once a mundane fact of life and one of the most important acts we undertake. We might not wander for ten years in the Mediterranean or be confronted with talking cats (Cheshire or otherwise), but we are always transformed in the process. To do so we must abandon a part of our old selves. In this sense leaving home alters both our sense of who exactly is doing the leaving and what exactly is left behind.

Leaving home can be baffling, challenging, exhilarating, painful, liberating, irritating and much else besides. This anthology is designed to address some of the difficulties and confusions that our departure poses.

There's the trouble of setting out in the first place, which is covered in the opening section of this anthology, 'On Going on a Journey'. Classic authors such as the renowned essayist William Hazlitt and unfairly ignored writers such as Rose Macaulay discuss the difficulties around setting off, helping us reflect on our reasons for leaving home.

We might, in leaving home, find a new one for ourselves. We may later return and discover that our home no longer exists – not as we remember it, not as it was, because we have changed and it has changed along with the people in it. We might discover, as T. S. Eliot suggests, that the end of our explorations is arriving where we started and knowing the place for the first time. Or we might wish to remain nomadic and keep roving across the world, that 'pleasure garden or paradise in which we may wander at large', in Rose Macaulay's words.

Once we've left home, we must deal with what we encounter along the way – that's the section on 'coping'. Pioneering explorers of the globe and the human soul such as the daring adventurer Gertrude Bell and acclaimed Scottish writer Robert Louis Stevenson discuss the challenges of independence and what becomes of us along the way. The Roman philosopher Seneca teaches us how to master ourselves and see in our own departure the opportunities that await.

We cannot know what will become of us after we leave home. We do know, however, what will most likely happen if we stay. There is a reason why leaving home is associated throughout world literature with voyages of rebirth and self-discovery. In the hero's journey the first major step is to cross the threshold of the known and venture forth into the unfamiliar – in other words, not everyone who leaves home becomes a hero, but every hero must leave home.

In the final section, poets, philosophers and sages discuss the problem of finding our own path. American literary giants Mark Twain,

Henry David Thoreau and Walt Whitman knew that there would always be temptations to remain as we are. They also knew that we might forever long for a happy return to the past, to our old selves, or to the places and people that we have loved. Dorothy knew too that there's no place like home. But she could only find her path outside of Kansas – even the road that would take her home.

Like the tales of Odysseus, Don Quixote and Alice before her, Dorothy's story ends once she returns home. This is because from Gilgamesh onwards – since the first records of human storytelling – we've been interested in the odyssey, in what happens to us beyond the boundaries of what we know, after we leave home; we've been interested in the courage that it takes, the ambition and the sacrifice, whether it be for a pilgrimage or in exile, as a rite of passage or a quest, to find old friends or make new ones, or out of a simple desire to cultivate ourselves and grow.

In all these stories – from Odysseus to Alice, Don Quixote to Dorothy – each hero eventually finds their path, distinct and distinctly theirs. With the help of their examples and the wisdom in this book, you'll undoubtedly find your own.

On Going
on a Journey

WILLIAM HAZLITT

On Going a Journey

One of the pleasantest things in the world is going a journey; but I like to go by myself. I can enjoy society in a room; but out of doors, nature is company enough for me. I am then never less alone than when alone.

The fields his study, nature was his book.

I cannot see the wit of walking and talking at the same time. When I am in the country, I wish to vegetate like the country, I am not for criticising hedge-rows and black cattle. I go out of town in order to forget the town and all that is in it. There are those who for this purpose go to watering-places, and carry the metropolis with them. I like more elbow-room, and fewer incumbrances. I like solitude, when I give myself up to it, for the sake of solitude; nor do I ask for

——a friend in my retreat,
Whom I may whisper solitude is sweet.

The soul of a journey is liberty, perfect liberty, to think, feel, do just as one pleases. We go a journey chiefly to be free of all impediments and of all inconveniences; to leave ourselves behind, much more to get rid of others. It is because I want a little breathing-space to muse on indifferent matters, where Contemplation

May plume her feathers and let grow her
    wings,
That in the various bustle of resort
Were all too ruffled, and sometimes
    impair'd,

that I absent myself from the town for awhile, without feeling at a loss the moment I am left by myself. Instead of a friend in a post-chaise or in a Tilbury, to exchange good things with, and vary the same stale topics over again, for once let me have a truce with impertinence. Give me the clear blue sky over my head, and the green turf beneath my feet, a winding road before me, and a three hours' march to dinner—and then to thinking! It is hard if I cannot start some game on these lone heaths. I laugh, I run, I leap, I sing for joy. From the point of yonder rolling cloud, I plunge into my past being, and revel there, as the sunburnt Indian plunges headlong into the wave that wafts him to his native shore. Then long-forgotten things, like 'sunken wrack and sumless treasuries,' burst upon my eager sight, and I begin to feel, think, and be myself again. Instead of an awkward silence, broken by attempts at wit or dull common-places, mine is that undisturbed silence of the heart which alone is perfect eloquence. No one likes puns, alliterations, antitheses, argument, and analysis better than I do; but I sometimes had rather be without them. 'Leave, oh, leave me to my repose!' I have just now other business in hand, which would seem idle to you, but is with me 'very stuff of the conscience.' Is not this wild rose sweet without a comment? Does not this daisy leap to my heart set in its coat of emerald? Yet if I were to explain to you the circumstance that has so endeared it to me, you would only smile. Had I not better then keep it to myself, and let it serve me to brood over, from here to yonder craggy point and from thence onward to the far-distant horizon? I should be but bad company all that way, and therefore prefer being alone. I have heard it said that you may, when the moody fit comes on, walk or ride on by yourself, and indulge your reveries. But this looks like a breach of manners, a neglect of others, and you are thinking all the time that you ought to rejoin your party. 'Out upon such half-faced fellowship,' say I. I like to be either entirely to myself, or entirely at the disposal of others; to talk or be silent, to walk or sit still, to be sociable or solitary. I was pleased with an observation of Mr Cobbett's, that 'he thought it a bad French custom to drink our wine with our meals, and that an Englishman ought to do only one thing at a time.' So I cannot talk and think, or indulge in melancholy musing and lively conversation by fits and starts. 'Let me have a companion of my way,' says Sterne, 'were it but to remark how the shadows lengthen as the sun declines.' It is beautifully said: but in my opinion, this continual comparing of notes interferes with the involuntary impression of things upon the mind, and hurts the sentiment. If you only hint what you feel in a kind of dumb show, it is insipid: if you have to explain it, it is making a toil of a pleasure. You cannot read the book of nature, without being perpetually put to the trouble of translating it for the benefit of others. I am for the synthetical method on a journey, in preference to the analytical. I am content to lay in a stock of ideas then, and to examine and anatomise them afterwards. I want to see my vague notions float like the down of the thistle before the breeze, and not to have them entangled in the briars and thorns of controversy. For once, I like to have it all my own way; and this is impossible unless you are alone, or in such company as I do not covet. I have no objection to argue a point with any one for twenty miles of measured road, but not for pleasure. If you remark the scent of a beanfield crossing the road, perhaps your fellow-traveller has no smell. If you point to a distant object, perhaps he is short-sighted, and has to take out his glass to look at it. There is a feeling in the air, a tone in the colour of a cloud which hits your fancy, but the effect of which you are unable to account for. There is then no sympathy, but an uneasy craving after it, and a dissatisfaction which pursues you on the way, and in the end probably produces ill humour. Now I never quarrel with myself, and take all my own conclusions for granted till I find it necessary to defend them against objections. It is not merely that you may not be of accord on the objects and circumstances that present them-selves before you—these may recall a number of objects, and lead to associations too delicate and refined to be possibly communicated to others. Yet these I love to cherish, and sometimes still fondly clutch them, when I can escape from the throng to do so. To give way to our feelings before company, seems extravagance or affectation; and on the other hand, to have to unravel this mystery of our being at every turn, and to make others take an equal interest in it (otherwise the end is not answered) is a task to which few are competent. We must 'give it an understanding, but no tongue.' My old friend C——, however, could do both. He could go on in the most delightful explanatory way over hill and dale, a summer's day, and convert a landscape into a didactic poem or a Pindaric ode. 'He talked far above singing.' If I could so clothe my ideas in sounding and flowing words, I might perhaps wish to have some one with me to admire the swelling theme; or I could be more content, were it possible for me still to hear his echoing voice in the woods of All-Foxden. They had 'that fine madness in them which our first poets had'; and if they could have been caught by some rare instrument, would have breathed such strains as the following.

——Here be woods as green
As any, air likewise as fresh and sweet

As when smooth Zephyrus plays on the fleet
Face of the curled stream, with flow'rs
   as many
As the young spring gives, and as choice
   as any;
Here be all new delights, cool streams
   and wells,
Arbours o'ergrown with woodbine, caves
   and dells;
Choose where thou wilt, while I sit by
   and sing,
Or gather rushes to make many a ring
For thy long fingers; tell thee tales of love,
How the pale Phoebe, hunting in a grove,
First saw the boy Endymion, from
   whose eyes
She took eternal fire that never dies;
How she convey'd him softly in a sleep,
His temples bound with poppy, to the steep
Head of old Latmos, where she stoops
   each night,
Gilding the mountain with her brother's light,
To kiss her sweetest.——

               FAITHFUL SHEPHERDESS.

Had I words and images at command like these,
I would attempt to wake the thoughts that lie

slumbering on golden ridges in the evening clouds: but at the sight of nature my fancy, poor as it is, droops and closes up its leaves, like flowers at sunset. I can make nothing out on the spot:—I must have time to collect myself.—

In general, a good thing spoils out-of-door prospects: it should be reserved for Table-talk. L——is for this reason, I take it, the worst company in the world out of doors; because he is the best within. I grant, there is one subject on which it is pleasant to talk on a journey; and that is, what one shall have for supper when we get to our inn at night. The open air improves this sort of conversation or friendly altercation, by setting a keener edge on appetite. Every mile of the road heightens the flavour of the viands we expect at the end of it. How fine it is to enter some old town, walled and turreted, just at the approach of night-fall, or to come to some straggling village, with the lights streaming through the surrounding gloom; and then after inquiring for the best entertainment that the place affords, to 'take one's ease at one's inn!' These eventful moments in our lives' history are too precious, too full of solid, heartfelt happiness to be frittered and dribbled away in imperfect sympathy. I would have them all to myself, and drain them to the last drop: they will do to talk of or to write about afterwards. What a delicate speculation it is, after drinking whole goblets of tea,

The cups that cheer, but not inebriate,

and letting the fumes ascend into the brain, to sit considering what we shall have for supper—eggs and a rasher, a rabbit smothered in onions, or an excellent veal-cutlet! Sancho in such a situation once fixed upon cow-heel; and his choice, though he could not help it, is not to be disparaged. Then in the intervals of pictured scenery and Shandean contemplation, to catch the preparation and the stir in the kitchen—*Procul, O procul este profani!* These hours are sacred to silence and to musing, to be treasured up in the memory, and to feed the source of smiling thoughts hereafter. I would not waste them in idle talk; or if I must have the integrity of fancy broken in upon, I would rather it were by a stranger than a friend. A stranger takes his hue and character from the time and place; he is a part of the furniture and costume of an inn. If he is a Quaker, or from the West Riding of Yorkshire, so much the better. I do not even try to sympathise with him, and he breaks no squares. I associate nothing with my travelling companion but present objects and passing events. In his ignorance of me and my affairs, I in a manner forget myself. But a friend reminds one of other things, rips up old grievances, and destroys the abstraction of the scene. He comes in ungraciously between us and our imaginary character. Something is dropped in the course of conversation that gives a hint of your profession and pursuits; or from having some one with you that knows the less sublime portions of your history, it seems that other people do. You are no longer a citizen of the world: but your 'unhoused free condition is put into circumscription and confine.' The *incognito* of an inn is one of its striking privileges—'lord of one's-self, uncumber'd with a name.' Oh! it is great to shake off the trammels of the world and of public opinion—to lose our importunate, tormenting, everlasting personal identity in the elements of nature, and become the creature of the moment, clear of all ties—to hold to the universe only by a dish of sweetbreads, and to owe nothing but the score of the evening—and no longer seeking for applause and meeting with contempt, to be known by no other title than *the Gentleman in the parlour!* One may take one's choice of all characters in this romantic state of uncertainty as to one's real pretensions, and become indefinitely respectable and negatively right-worshipful. We baffle prejudice and disappoint conjecture; and from being so to others, begin to be objects of curiosity and wonder even to ourselves. We are no more those hackneyed common-places that we appear in the world: an inn restores us to the level of nature, and quits scores with society! I have certainly spent some enviable hours at inns—sometimes when I have been left entirely to myself, and have tried to solve some metaphysical problem, as once at Witham-common, where I found out the proof that likeness is not a case of the association of ideas—at other times, when there have been pictures in the room, as at St Neot's (I think it was), where I first met with Gribelin's engravings of the Cartoons, into which I entered at once, and at a little inn on the borders of Wales, where there happened to be hanging some of Westall's drawings, which I compared triumphantly (for a theory that I had, not for the admired artist) with the figure of a girl who had ferried me over the Severn, standing up in the boat between me and the twilight—at other times I might mention luxuriating in books, with a peculiar interest in this way, as I remember sitting up half the night to read Paul and Virginia, which I picked up at an inn at Bridgewater, after being drenched in the rain all day; and at the same place I got through two volumes of Madame D'Arblay's Camilla. It was on the tenth of April, 1798, that I sat down to a volume of the New Eloise, at the inn at Llangollen, over a bottle of sherry and a cold chicken. The letter I chose was that in which St Preux describes his feelings as he caught a glimpse from the heights of the Jura of the Pays de Vaud, which I had brought with me as a *bonne bouche* to crown the evening with. It was my birth-day, and I had for the first time come from a place in the neighbourhood to visit this delightful spot. The road to Llangollen turns off between Chirk and Wrexham; and on passing a certain point, you come all at once upon the valley, which opens like an amphitheatre, broad, barren hills rising in majestic state on either side, with 'green upland swells that echo to the bleat of flocks' below, and the river Dee babbling over its stony bed in the midst of them. The valley at this time 'glittered green with sunny showers,' and a budding ash-tree dipped its tender branches in the chiding stream. How proud, how glad I was to walk along the high road that overlooks the delicious prospect, repeating the lines which I have just quoted from Mr Coleridge's poems! But besides the prospect which opened beneath my feet, another also opened to my inward sight, a heavenly vision, on which were written, in letters large as Hope could make them, these four words, LIBERTY, GENIUS, LOVE, VIRTUE; which have since faded into the light of common day, or mock my idle gaze.

The beautiful is vanished, and returns not.

Still I would return some time or other to this enchanted spot; but I would return to it alone. What other self could I find to share that influx of thoughts, of regret, and delight, the fragments of which I could hardly conjure up to myself, so much have they been broken and defaced! I could stand on some tall rock, and overlook the precipice of years that separates me from what I then was. I was at that time going shortly to visit the poet whom I have above named. Where is he now? Not only I myself have changed; the world, which was then new to me, has become old and incorrigible. Yet will I turn to thee in thought, O sylvan Dee, in joy, in youth and gladness as thou then wert; and thou shalt always be to me the river of Paradise, where I will drink of the waters of life freely!

There is hardly any thing that shows the

short-sightedness or capriciousness of the imagination more than travelling does. With change of place we change our ideas; nay, our opinions and feelings. We can by an effort indeed transport ourselves to old and long-forgotten scenes, and then the picture of the mind revives again; but we forget those that we have just left. It seems that we can think but of one place at a time. The canvas of the fancy is but of a certain extent, and if we paint one set of objects upon it, they immediately efface every other. We cannot enlarge our conceptions, we only shift our point of view. The landscape bares its bosom to the enraptured eye, we take our fill of it, and seem as if we could form no other image of beauty or grandeur. We pass on, and think no more of it: the horizon that shuts it from our sight, also blots it from our memory like a dream. In travelling through a wild barren country, I can form no idea of a woody and cultivated one. It appears to me that all the world must be barren, like what I see of it. In the country we forget the town, and in town we despise the country; 'Beyond Hyde Park,' says Sir Fopling Flutter, 'all is a desert.' All that part of the map that we do not see before us is a blank. The world in our conceit of it is not much bigger than a nutshell.

It is not one prospect expanded into another, county joined to county, kingdom to kingdom, lands to seas, making an image voluminous and vast;—the mind can form no larger idea of space than the eye can take in at a single glance. The rest is a name written in a map, a calculation of arithmetic. For instance, what is the true signification of that immense mass of territory and population, known by the name of China to us? An inch of paste-board on a wooden globe, of no more account than a China orange! Things near us are seen of the size of life: things at a distance are diminished to the size of the understanding. We measure the universe by ourselves, and even comprehend the texture of our own being only piece-meal. In this way, however, we remember an infinity of things and places. The mind is like a mechanical instrument that plays a great variety of tunes, but it must play them in succession. One idea recalls another, but it at the same time excludes all others. In trying to renew old recollections, we cannot as it were unfold the whole web of our existence; we must pick out the single threads. So in coming to a place where we have formerly lived and with which we have intimate associations, every one must have found that the feeling grows more vivid the nearer we approach the spot, from the mere anticipation of the actual impression: we remember circumstances, feelings, persons, faces, names, that we had not thought of for years; but for the time all the rest of the world is forgotten!—To return to the question I have quitted above.

I have no objection to go to see ruins, aqueducts, pictures, in company with a friend or a party, but rather the contrary, for the former reason reversed. They are intelligible matters, and will bear talking about. The sentiment here is not tacit, but communicable and overt. Salisbury Plain is barren of criticism, but Stonehenge will bear a discussion antiquarian, picturesque, and philosophical. In setting out on a party of pleasure, the first consideration always is where we shall go to: in taking a solitary ramble, the question is what we shall meet with by the way. 'The mind is its own place'; nor are we anxious to arrive at the end of our journey. I can myself do the honours indifferently well to works of art and curiosity. I once took a party to Oxford with no mean *éclat*— shewed them that seat of the Muses at a distance,

With glistering spires and pinnacles
    adorn'd—

descanted on the learned air that breathes from the grassy quadrangles and stone walls of halls and colleges—was at home in the Bodleian; and at Blenheim quite superseded the powdered Cicerone that attended us, and that pointed in vain with his wand to common-place beauties in matchless pictures.—As another exception to the above reasoning, I should not feel confident in venturing on a journey in a foreign country without a companion. I should want at intervals to hear the sound of my own language. There is an involuntary antipathy in the mind of an Englishman to foreign manners and notions that requires the assistance of social sympathy to carry it off. As the distance from home increases, this relief, which was at first a luxury, becomes a passion and an appetite. A person would almost feel stifled to find himself in the deserts of Arabia without friends and countrymen: there must be allowed to be something in the view of Athens or old Rome that claims the utterance of speech; and I own that the Pyramids are too mighty for any single contemplation. In such situations, so opposite to all one's ordinary train of ideas, one seems a species by one's-self, a limb torn off from society, unless one can meet with instant fellowship and support.—Yet I did not feel this want or craving very pressing once, when I first set my foot on the laughing shores of France. Calais was peopled with novelty and delight. The confused, busy murmur of the place was like oil and wine poured into my ears; nor did the mariners' hymn, which was sung from the top of an old crazy vessel in the harbour, as the sun went down, send an alien sound into my soul. I only breathed the air of general humanity. I walked over 'the vine-covered hills and gay regions of France,' erect and satisfied; for the image of man was not cast down and chained to the foot of arbitrary thrones: I was at no loss for language, for that of all the great schools of painting was open to me. The whole is vanished like a shade. Pictures, heroes, glory, freedom, all are fled: nothing remains but the Bourbons and the French people!—There is undoubtedly a sensation in travelling into foreign parts that is to be had nowhere else: but it is more pleasing at the time than lasting. It is too remote from our habitual associations to be a common topic of discourse or reference, and, like a dream or another state of existence, does not piece into our daily modes of life. It is an animated but a momentary hallucination. It demands an effort to exchange our actual for our ideal identity; and to feel the pulse of our old transports revive very keenly, we must 'jump' all our present comforts and connexions. Our romantic and itinerant character is not to be domesticated. Dr Johnson remarked how little foreign travel added to the facilities of conversation in those who had been abroad. In fact, the time we have spent there is both delightful and in one sense instructive; but it appears to be cut out of our substantial, downright existence, and never to join kindly on to it. We are not the same, but another, and perhaps more enviable individual, all the time we are out of our own country. We are lost to ourselves, as well as our friends. So the poet somewhat quaintly sings,

Out of my country and myself I go.

Those who wish to forget painful thoughts, do well to absent themselves for a while from the ties and objects that recall them: but we can be said only to fulfil our destiny in the place that gave us birth. I should on this account like well enough to spend the whole of my life in travelling abroad, if I could any where borrow another life to spend afterwards at home!—

HILAIRE BELLOC

On Discovery

There is a great consolation lying all bottled and matured for those who choose to take it, in the modern world—and yet how few turn to it and drink the bracing draught! It is a consolation for dust and frequency and fatigue and despair—this consolation is the Discovery of the World.

The world has no end to it. You can discover one town which you had thought well known, or one quarter of the town, or one house in the quarter of the town, or the room in that house, or one picture in that room. The avenues of discovery open out infinite in number and quite a little distance from their centre (which is yourself and your local, tired, repeated experience). these avenues diverge outwards and lend to the most amazingly different things.

You can take some place of which you have

heard so often and in so vulgar a connotation that you could wish never to hear of it again, and coming there you will find it holding you, and you will enjoy many happy surprises, unveiling things you could not dream were there.

How much more true is it not, then, that discovery awaits you if you will take the least little step off the high road, or the least little exploration into the past of a place you visit.

Most men inhabiting a countryside know nothing of its aspect even quite close to their homes, save as it is seen from the main roads. If they will but cross a couple of fields or so, they may come, for the first time in many years of habitation, upon a landscape that seems quite new and a sight of their own hills which makes them look like the hills of a strange country.

In youth we all know this. In youth and early manhood we wonder what is behind some rise of land, or on the other side of some wood which bounded our horizon in childhood. Then comes a day when we manfully explore the unknown places and go to find what we shall find.

As life advances we imagine that all this chance of discovery has been taken from us by our increased experience. It is an illusion. If we are so dull it is we that have changed and not the world; and what is more we can recover from that dullness, and there is a simple medicine for it, which is to repeat the old experiment: to go out and see what we may see.

Some will grant this true of the sudden little new discoveries quite close to home, but not of travel. Travel, they think, must always be to-day by some known road to some known place, with dust upon the mind at the setting out and at the coming in. It is a great error. You can choose some place too famous in Europe and even too peopled and too large, and yet make the most ample discoveries there.

"Oh, but," a man will say, "most places have been so written of that one knows them already long before seeing them."

No: one does nothing of the kind. Even the pictured and the storied places are full enough of newness if one will but shake off routine and if one will but peer.

Speak to five men of some place which they have all visited, perhaps together, and find out what each noticed most: you will be amazed at the five different impressions.

Enter by some new entry a town which hitherto you had always entered by one fixed way, and again vary your entry, and again, and you will see a new town every time.

There are many, many thousand Englishmen who know the wonderful sight of Rouen from the railway bridge below the town, for that lies on the high road to Paris, and there are many thousand, though not so many, who know Rouen from Bon-Secours. There are a few hundred who know it from the approach by the great woods to the North. There are a dozen or so perhaps who have come in from the East, walking from Picardy. The great town lying in its cup of hills is quite different every way.

There is a view of Naples which has been photographed and printed and painted until we are all tired of it. It is a view taken from the hill which makes the northern horn of the Bay; there is a big pine tree in the foreground and Vesuvius smoking in the background, and I will bargain that most people who read this have seen that view upon a postcard, or in a shop window, and that a good many of them would rightly say that it was the most hackneyed thing in Europe.

Now some years ago I had occasion to go to Naples, a town I had always avoided for that very reason—that one heard of it until one was tired and that this view had become like last year's music hall tunes.

I went, not of my own choice but because I had to go, and when I got there I made as complete a discovery as ever Columbus made or those sailors who first rounded Africa and found the Indian Seas.

Naples was utterly unlike anything I had imagined. Vesuvius was not a cone smoking upon the horizon—it was a great angry pyramid toppling right above me. The town was not a lazy, dirty town with all the marks of antiquity and none of energy. It was alive with commerce and all the evils and all the good of commerce. It was angrily alive; it was like a wasp nest.

I will state the plain truth at the risk of being thought paradoxical. Naples recalled to me an *American* seaboard town so vividly that I could have thought myself upon the Pacific. I could have gone on for days digging into all this new experience, turning it over and fructifying it. My business allowed me not twenty-four hours, but the vision was one I shall never forget, and it was as completely new and as wholly creative, or re-creative, of the mind, as is that land-fall which an adventurous sailor makes when he finds a new island at dawn upon a sea not yet travelled.

Every one, therefore, should go out to discover, five miles from home, or five hundred. Every one should assure himself against the cheating tedium which books and maps create in us, that the world is perpetually new: and oddly enough it is not a matter of money.

ROSE MACAULAY

Abroad

The great and recurrent question about Abroad is, is it worth the trouble of getting there? Delicious as is the prospect we see beyond this travail, shall we be enabled to conquer sloth's enticements, and emerge from what Mr. Thomas Coryat, that enterprising Jacobean tourist, contemptuously termed our domestical lurking corners? Is there any peace, the voice of indolence protests, in ever climbing up the climbing wave?

Let us hearken rather to the stirring exhortations of Mr. Coryat, who must have been minded much like Mr. Thomas Cook, and spoke with his very accents. "Let us," cried Mr. Coryat, "propose before our eyes that most beautiful theatre of the universe, let us behold whatever is abroad in the world, let us look into provinces, see cities, run over kingdoms and empires. Surely we shall find," said he, hopefully, "those people which have used no journeys to be rude, slothful, uncivil, rough, outrageous, foolish, barbarous, void of all humanity, civility and courteous entertainment, proud, arrogant, puffed up with self love and admiration of themselves, also effeminate, wanton, given to sleep, banquetings, dice and idleness, corrupted with the allurements of all pleasures and the enticements of all concupiscence."

But this is getting to sound agreeable; if home offers all that, one might do worse than stay there. Our tourist perceives this, and hurries on in different vein: "Such is the sweetness of travelling and seeing the world, such the pleasure, such the delight, that I think that man void of all sense and of a stony hardness, which cannot be moved with so great a pleasure . . . O sluggish, abject, servile, and most dejected mind, which includeth itself within the narrow bounds of his own house."

Perhaps it is the expense you dread? "As though the dice and dicing box, domestical idleness, domestical luxury, and the gulf of domestical gourmandizing, doth not far exceed the necessary charges of travel."

That is as may be. Perhaps one would do well not to balance the nicely calculated less and more, but to remember the spring cleaning, or the house painting, and consider how many by their travels have procured themselves evasion from domestical calamities and miseries.

Arise, then, from abject and home-keeping sloth. Cease to regard with effeminate distaste those hurdles which stand between you and Abroad, looming high, barred, enthorned, only by the strong to be o'er-leapt. Do tickets, passports, money, travellers' cheques, packing, reservations, boat trains, inns, crouch and snarl before you like those surly dragons that guard enchanted lands? A little firmness, a nice mingling of industry, negligence and guile, and the hurdles will be leaped, the dragons passed; snapping your fingers at what you have left undone, you launch yourself into space.

Yes, you are on the boat train; you make once more the Grand Tour; you are full steam ahead for Dover, for Boulogne, for the silver seas whereon trumpet and pipe these enticing sirens against whose penetrating call even Ulysses would have cered his ears in vain. Hola, Captain! where is the packet for France? Here, Sir, here, and a fair wind in our sails. Honest gentlemen who will for Calais, let them make haste. To Calais ho! Aboard ho! The wind is at North, North, and North-West. Is the ship well armed, Captain? Fear nothing, Sir, for the ship is very well equipped with artillery and munition. Go into the prow. The wind blows, the tide swells, see the waves mount. The sea begins to rise and rage from the very bottom. See how those huge waves beat against the sides of our ship. Hear you these terrible whirlwinds, how they sing over our sailyards? We shall have by and by a storm. The tempest makes a great noise. The heaven begins to thunder from above. It thunders, it lightens, it rains, it hails; it is best to strike sail, and to veer the cables. This wave will carry us to all the Devils . . . O my friends on shore! O thrice and four times happy are those who are on firm land setting of beans! O St. James, St. Peter, and St. Christopher! O St. Michael, St. Nicholas! O God we are now at the bottom of the sea. I give eighteen hundred thousand crowns to him who will set me a land. Let's land, let's go a shore. Captain, I will give you all that I have in the world to set me a shore. Will you go a shore in the midst of the ocean sea, Sir? What a horrible tempest! By St. Grison what means this? Shall we take our sepulture here among these waves? I pardon all the world. I die, my friends. Fare you all well.

The tempest is now ended. Oh, it is fine weather again. A fig for the waves. We are in the haven of Calais. We are saved. Cannoneer, shoot off a piece of artillery. Les passeports, s'il vous plaît. Oh, yes, indeed, anything. Par ici pour la douane. By all means yes, even that. How delighted I am to be arrived! Here is all my luggage, and all its keys.

Yes, you may look at everything, tumble everything about. No, nothing to declare, nothing at all; still, by all means rummage. This one too? Of course. And now you will chalk them; that is nice. Now for the train; allons, allons, facteur! Second-class, n'est-ce-pas. No, nothing else about it matters, and I have no reserved seat. Put me anywhere. What? All reserved? Then I must wait for another train, n'est-ce-pas. No, I never reserve seats in advance, it is quite too much trouble. What I say is, why make a business of what is meant for a pleasure? If a railway ticket does not get me on to a French train, then France is not the land of liberty, equality, or fraternity. But then, one never supposed that it was. There will be another train presently, free to all? That is excellent news. I will settle down; I will wait. Attention, there is a train. Allons, allons, facteur; deuxième classe, s'il vous plaît. Ah, Ah, I am on the train, n'est-ce-pas. Mettez mes bagages on the rack, on the seat, on the floor, all about me. Je suis bien entourèe, n'est-ce-pas. But see, there lacks one bagage; where can it be? Oh, Oh, you have left it on the platform over there. Vite, vite, facteur! The train departs. You have not been vite enough; the train is departed. I shall not see my bag again. Je me plaindrai au consul anglais.

Eh bien. Life is like that. Abroad, in particular, is like that. And now I am abroad; I am entrained; I am launched on my enchanting error across Europe. Where shall I go? France, Spain, Italy, everywhere; perhaps even Portugal. How fast and how loud foreigners talk! It is a gift; the British cannot talk so loud or so fast. They have too many centuries of fog in their throats. Besides, they are nervous; they dare not talk loud; they mumble and murmur, afraid lest some one will hear. Never mind them; forget them; too many of them are, indeed, on this train, on all trains, since the English cannot keep still or stay at home, but still we will ignore and forget them, we will feign that we are alone abroad among the foreigners. Allons, allons, mes braves compagnons! To Paris ho! But only to make a change of train; we will not linger in Paris, it is drab and cold. Across it quickly to the Gare de Lyons, the Gare d'Orléans, and off to the South. East or west, Marseilles or Bordeaux, Mediterranean or Atlantic, Italy or Spain, it matters not, it is all south. Palms, pines, pepper, eucalyptus, oranges, lemons, juniper, myrtle; Alps, Apennines, Pyrenees; Basque, Catalan, Castilian, Mallorquin, Ligurian, Tuscan, Sicilian, Venetian, Greek, Portuguese—any language you like, I have the phrase-books of some of them, and can do the rest by signs. To Greece with little English ladies and schoolmasters, questing after ancient Hellenes. *Αθήνα! Ολυμπία!* To Athens! To Olympia! *Αθηναιείσι καλαί.* Athens are beautiful. Oh, how beautiful Athens are! That is to say, they are vulgar and modern and dirty, but never mind, we rummage among them, we find the Acropolis. Schoolmasters, dons, little eager ladies, we swarm about the Acropolis, among the modern Hellenes, who do not comprehend their own ancient tongue when we speak it to them, who desire only that we should give them money. Over the hills to Corinth; Greece is terra-cotta coloured, and silver with olives; tortoises and lizards scuttle over it. The Vale of Tempe is dark and deep, and Peneius shines in it like an agate. All the plains of Thessaly; Olympus, Ossa and Pelion; Thermopylæ, Parnassus, Thebes, Cithæron; the schoolmasters, the dons, the little ladies, are overwhelmed. Greece is really excessive. One cannot idle in it, or be stupid or inert, no, not for a moment, or one will miss something, one wastes one's time, since it is possible that one will not be this way again. One cannot, in Greece, be happy merely in being Abroad. For Abroad, Italy and France and Spain and Czecho-Slovakia and Scandinavia and the Americas and the South Seas are better. Back, then, to Italy; Sicily and Calabria and Naples; look how Vesuvius smokes! Stroll about Pompeii, so gay, so coloured, so still; if you are encouraging, one of the custodians will show you a house freshly dug, and perhaps embrace you in it. Rome, Florence, Siens, Umbria, Venice, the lakes; having seen all these, settle down on the Ligurian sea shore and bathe. Nothing to see here but sea and shore and fishermen and nets and mountains and some small town. No buildings, no pictures, no churches, nothing but Abroad. Buon giorno, signorina, sta bene oggi? Benissimo, grazie, signore; mi bagnerò nel mare, dopo di prendere il caffè. Caffè latte! how it froths into the thick white cup! Sugar tablets wrapped in paper, coarse white crusty roll, church bells clanging, fishermen shouting, small waves lisping on the sand. You can stay in the sea all day if you wish, coming out to dry and toast, and slipping in again. It is deep sky-blue, and there is a rock far out on which you can sit. Great Britain can give you buildings, picture galleries, cities, (though of no great moment and of inconsiderable antiquity) and scenery, but only Abroad can give you real bathing.

For that matter, only Abroad can provide a great deal else. Meals, for example, in the streets. Trams that blow horns; indeed, traffic horns in general play a sweeter, liltier music than ever they play in Britain. How their gay tune, on two notes, like a cuckoo's song reversed, lifts the heart! Mountains of a height, a jaggedness, a grandeur, that surpasses those of Caledonia, Westmorland and Wales. Terraces climbing up their lower slopes, set with olives, chestnuts, figs, and vines. Large white oxen drawing loads of marble. Mules drawing sand. Nets being hauled in from the sea heavy with bianchetti, and perhaps a tunny or two. Processions round the town, led by nasally chanting acolytes and magnificently dressed wax saints, and followed by the citizens. Rose petals scattered and flung from every window on to the Corpus Christi procession: Little St. John, the Baptist, his hair just released from a week's curling-papers, leading his unruly lamb in the procession on his day. Brown and beautiful Basques dancing the fandango in the squares after a pelota match on Sunday evening. Redwood forests, giant cactuses in a pale Arizona desert, palms and orange trees and futbal in the plaza, the great blue sweep of Mexican mountains, the brown adobe of Mexican villages, the yucca standing high like blossoming swords, the wild roads not mended since the last revolution, the tiny burros carrying Mexicans, the estancias, haciendas, chile con carne, tortillas, the comida con vino incluso, the mandolins twanging in the plaza while you sit on the pavement and eat. The hot dog stalls, the camping cabins, San Francisco on her hills above the Golden Gate, Santa Barbara in white adobe, set with lit fir-trees on a warm Christmas night, San Diego, Tia Juana, and the Old Spanish Trail. The Florida seas and their leaning palmettos, the Keys and their twisted mangroves, Cuba across the straits. A small Provencal estaminet on the foothills, a mountain road twisting above it. Sunshine and warmth, sunshine and warmth, and the scent of lemons on the air. And, naturally, foreigners. I do not prefer foreigners to the English, except that they speak another language. Otherwise they are, I find, essentially much the same, though the Italians and Spanish are handsomer and browner, and the Americans more cordial. But they all belong to Abroad, that great, that delightful

English picnic. So, like Walt Whitman, I make a salute to all foreigners. As he so exuberantly exclaimed, "You Sardinian, you Bavarian, Swabian, Saxon, Wallachian, Bulgarian! You Roman, Neapolitan, you Greek! You little Matador in the arena at Seville! You mountaineer living lawlessly on the Taurus or Caucasus! You thoughtful Armenian! You Japanese! All you continentals of Asia, Africa, Europe, Australia, indifferent of place! You benighted roamer of Amazonia! You Patagonian, you Feejeeman! . . . I do not say one word against you! Salut au monde!"

He was right. It is all Abroad, all that vast camping ground, pleasure garden or paradise in which we may wander at large; or might until recently, when passports, bureaucracy and suspicion are attempting to hamper and limit our tranquil and happy errors over our errant celestial ball. Les passeports s'il vous plait! Par ici pour la douane! Apra la sua valigia! Sin duda quejaré al consul ingles. I guess we'll have to put you on Ellis Island, if that's all the dollars you have.

Yes; we are hampered, invigilated, kept in on every side, very likely flung into gaol, directly we step into our pleasure-ground. But, when governments and their watch-dogs have done their worst, it is still Abroad.

Coping

SENECA THE YOUNGER

On Consolation to His Mother Helvia

I. My best of mothers, I have often felt eager to console you, and have as often checked that impulse. Many things urged me to make the attempt: in the first place, I thought that if, though I might not be able to restrain your tears, yet that if I could even wipe them away, I should set myself free from all my own sorrows: then I was quite sure that I should rouse you from your grief with more authority if I had first shaken it off myself. I feared, too, lest Fortune, though overcome by me, might nevertheless overcome some one of my family. Then I endeavoured to crawl and bind up your wounds in the best way I could, holding my hand over my own wound; but then again other considerations occurred to me which held me back: I knew that I must not oppose your grief during its first transports, lest my very attempts at consolation might irritate it, and add

43

fuel to it: for in diseases, also, there is nothing more hurtful than medicine applied too soon. I waited, therefore, until it exhausted itself by its own violence, and being weakened by time, so that it was able to bear remedies, would allow itself to be handled and touched. Beside this, while turning over all the works which the greatest geniuses have composed, for the purpose of soothing and pacifying grief, I could not find any instance of one who had offered consolation to his relatives, while he himself was being sorrowed over by them. Thus, the subject being a new one, I hesitated and feared that instead of consoling, I might embitter your grief. Then there was the thought that a man who had only just raised his head after burying his child, and who wished to console his friends, would require to use new phrases not taken from our common every-day words of comfort: but every sorrow of more than usual magnitude must needs prevent one's choosing one's words, seeing that it often prevents one's using one's very voice. However this may be, I will make the attempt, not trusting in my own genius, but because my consolation will be most powerful since it is I who offer it. You never would deny me anything, and I hope, though all grief is obstinate, that you will surely not refuse me this request, that you will allow me to set bounds to your sorrow.

II. See how far I have presumed upon your indulgence: I have no doubts about my having more power over you than your grief, than which nothing has more power over the unhappy. In order, therefore, to avoid encountering it straightway, I will at first take its part and offer it every encouragement: I will rip up and bring to light again wounds already scarred. Some one may say, "What sort of consolation is this, for a man to rake up buried evils, and to bring all its sorrows before a mind which scarcely can bear the sight of one?" but let him reflect that diseases which are so malignant that they do but gather strength from ordinary remedies, may often be cured by the opposite treatment: I will, therefore, display before your grief all its woes and miseries: this will be to effect a cure, not by soothing measures, but by cautery and the knife. What shall I gain by this? I shall make the mind that could overcome so many sorrows, ashamed to bewail one wound more in a body so full of scars. Let those whose feeble minds have been enervated by a long period of happiness, weep and lament for many days, and faint away on receiving the slightest blow: but those whose years have all been passed amid catastrophes should bear the severest losses with brave and unyielding patience. Continual misfortune has this one advantage, that it ends by rendering callous those whom it is always scourging. Ill fortune has given you no respite, and has not left even your birthday free from the bitterest grief: you lost your mother as soon as you were born, nay, while you were being born, and you came into life, as it were, an outcast: you grew up under a step-mother, whom you made into a mother by all the obedience and respect which even a real daughter could have bestowed upon her: and even a good step-mother costs every one dear. You lost your most affectionate uncle, a brave and excellent man, just when you were awaiting his return: and, lest Fortune should weaken its blows by dividing them, within a month you lost your beloved husband, by whom you had become the mother of three children. This sorrowful news was brought you while you were already in mourning, while all your children were absent, so that all your misfortunes seemed to have been purposely brought upon you at a time when your grief could nowhere find any repose. I pass over all the dangers and

alarms which you have endured without any respite: it was but the other day that you received
the bones of three of your grandchildren in the
bosom from which you had sent them forth: less
than twenty days after you had buried my child,
who perished in your arms and amid your kisses,
you heard that I had been exiled: you wanted only
this drop in your cup, to have to weep for those
who still lived.

III. The last wound is, I admit, the severest that
you have ever yet sustained: it has not merely
torn the skin, but has pierced you to the very
heart: yet as recruits cry aloud when only slightly
wounded, and shudder more at the hands of the
surgeon than at the sword, while veterans even
when transfixed allow their hurts to be dressed
without a groan, and as patiently as if they were
in some one else's body, so now you ought to
offer yourself courageously to be healed. Lay
aside lamentations and wailings, and all the usual
noisy manifestations of female sorrow: you have
gained nothing by so many misfortunes, if you
have not learned how to suffer. Now, do I seem
not to have spared you? nay, I have not passed

over any of your sorrows, but have placed them all together in a mass before you.

IV. I have done this by way of a heroic remedy: for I have determined to conquer this grief of yours, not merely to limit it; and I shall conquer it, I believe, if in the first place I can prove that I am not suffering enough to entitle me to be called unhappy, let alone to justify me in rendering my family unhappy: and, secondly, if I can deal with your case and prove that even your misfortune, which comes upon you entirely through me, is not a severe one.

The point to which I shall first address myself is that of which your motherly love longs to hear, I mean, that I am not suffering: if I can, I will make it clear to you that the events by which you think that I am overwhelmed, are not unendurable: if you cannot believe this, I at any rate shall be all the more pleased with myself for being happy under circumstances which could make most men miserable. You need not believe what others say about me: that you may not be puzzled by any uncertainty as to what to think, I distinctly tell you that I am not miserable: I will add, for your greater comfort, that it is not possible for me to be made miserable.

V. We are born to a comfortable position enough, if we do not afterwards lose it: the aim of Nature has been to enable us to live well without needing a vast apparatus to enable us to do so: every man is able by himself to make himself happy. External circumstances have very little importance either for good or for evil: the wise man is neither elated by prosperity nor depressed by adversity; for he has always endeavoured to depend chiefly upon himself and to derive all his joys from himself. Do I, then, call myself a wise man? far from it: for were I able to profess myself wise, I should not only say that I was not unhappy, but should avow myself to be the most fortunate of men, and to be raised almost to the level of a god: as it is, I have applied myself to the society of wise men, which suffices to lighten all sorrows, and, not being as yet able to rely upon my own strength, I have betaken myself for refuge to the camp of others, of those, namely, who can easily defend both themselves and their friends. They have ordered me always to stand as it were on guard, and to mark the attacks and charges of Fortune long before she delivers them; she is only terrible to those whom she catches unawares; he who is always looking out for her assault, easily sustains it: for so also an invasion of the enemy overthrows those by whom it is unexpected, but those who have prepared themselves for the coming war before it broke out, stand in their ranks fully equipped and repel with ease the first, which is always the most furious onset. I never have trusted in Fortune, even when she seemed most peaceful. I have accepted all the gifts of wealth, high office, and influence, which she has so bountifully bestowed upon me, in such a manner that she can take them back again without disturbing me: I have kept a great distance between them and myself: and therefore she has taken them, not painfully torn them away from me. No man loses anything by the frowns of Fortune unless he has been deceived by her smiles: those who have enjoyed her bounty as though it were their own heritage for ever, and who have chosen to take precedence of others because of it, lie in abject sorrow when her unreal and fleeting delights forsake their empty childish minds, that know nothing about solid pleasure: but he who has not been puffed up by success, does not collapse after failure: he possesses a mind of tried constancy, superior to the influences of either state; for even in the midst of prosperity he has experimented upon his powers of enduring adversity. Consequently I have always believed that there was no real good in any of those things which all men desire: I then found that they were empty, and merely painted over with artificial and deceitful dyes, without containing anything within which corresponds to their outside: I now find nothing so harsh and fearful as the common opinion of mankind threatened me with in this which is known as adversity: the word itself, owing to the prevalent belief and ideas current about it, strikes somewhat unpleasantly upon one's ears, and thrills the hearers as something dismal and accursed, for so hath the vulgar decreed that it should be: but a great many of the decrees of the vulgar are reversed by the wise.

VI. Setting aside, then, the verdict of the majority, who are carried away by the first appearance of things and the usual opinion about them, let us consider what is meant by exile: clearly a changing from one place to another. That I may not seem to be narrowing its force, and taking away its worst parts, I must add, that this changing of place is accompanied by poverty, disgrace, and contempt. Against these I will combat later on: meanwhile I wish to consider what there is unpleasant in the mere act of changing one's place of abode.

"It is unbearable," men say, "to lose one's native land." Look, I pray you, on these vast crowds, for whom all the countless roofs of Rome can scarcely find shelter: the greater part of those crowds have lost their native land: they have flocked hither from their country towns and colonies, and in fine from all parts of the world. Some have been brought by ambition, some by the exigencies of public office, some by being entrusted with embassies, some by luxury which seeks a convenient spot, rich in vices, for its exercise, some by their wish for a liberal education, others by a wish to see the public shows. Some have been led hither by friendship, some by industry, which finds here a wide field for the display of its powers. Some have brought their beauty for sale, some their eloquence: people of every kind assemble themselves together in Rome, which sets a high price both upon virtues and vices. Bid them all to be summoned to answer to their names, and ask each one from what home he has come: you will find that the greater part of them have left their own abodes, and journeyed to a city which, though great and beauteous beyond all others, is nevertheless not their own. Then leave this city, which may be said to be the common property of all men, and visit all other towns: there is not one of them which does not contain a large proportion of aliens. Pass away from those whose delightful situation and convenient position attracts many settlers: examine wildernesses and the most rugged islands, Sciathus and Seriphus, Gyarus and Corsica: you will find no place of exile where some one does not dwell for his own pleasure. What can be found barer or more precipitous on every side than this rock? what more barren in respect of food? what more uncouth in its inhabitants? more mountainous in its configuration? or more rigorous in its climate? yet even here there are more strangers than natives. So far, therefore, is the mere change of place from being irksome, that even this place has allured some away from their country. I find some writers who declare that mankind has a natural itch for change of abode and alteration of domicile: for the mind of man is wandering and unquiet; it never stands still, but spreads itself abroad and sends forth its thoughts into all regions, known or unknown; being nomadic, impatient of repose, and loving novelty beyond everything else. You need not be suprised at this, if you reflect upon its original source: it is not formed from the same elements as the heavy and earthly body, but from heavenly spirit: now heavenly things are by their nature always in motion, speeding along and flying with the greatest swiftness. Look at the luminaries which light the world: none of them stands still. The sun is perpetually in motion, and passes from one quarter to another, and although he revolves with the entire heaven, yet nevertheless he has a motion in the contrary direction to that of the universe itself, and passes through all the constellations without remaining in any: his wandering is incessant, and he never ceases to move from place to place. All things continually revolve and are for ever changing; they pass from one position to another in accordance with natural and unalterable laws: after they have completed a certain circuit in a fixed space of time, they begin again the path which they had previously trodden. Be not surprised, then, if the human mind, which is formed from the same seeds as the heavenly bodies, delights in change and wandering, since the divine nature itself either takes pleasure in constant and exceeding swift motion or perhaps even preserves its existence thereby.

VII. Come now, turn from divine to human affairs: you will see that whole tribes and nations have changed their abodes. What is the meaning of Greek cities in the midst of barbarous districts? or of the Macedonian language existing among the Indians and the Persians? Scythia and all that region which swarms with wild and uncivilized tribes boasts nevertheless Achaean cities along the shores of the Black Sea. Neither the rigours of eternal winter, nor the character of men as savage as their climate, has prevented people migrating thither. There is a mass of Athenians in Asia Minor. Miletus has sent out into various parts of the world citizens enough to populate seventy-five cities. That whole coast of Italy which is washed by the Lower Sea is a part of what once was "Greater Greece." Asia claims the Tuscans as her own: there are Tyrians living in Africa, Carthaginians in Spain; Greeks have pushed in among the Gauls, and Gauls among the Greeks. The Pyrenees have proved no barrier to the Germans: human caprice makes its way through pathless and unknown regions: men drag along with them their children, their wives, and their aged and worn-out parents. Some have been tossed hither and thither by long wanderings, until they have become too wearied to choose an abode, but have settled in whatever place was nearest to them: others have made themselves masters of foreign countries by force of arms: some nations while making for parts unknown have been swallowed up by the sea: some have established themselves in the place in which they were originally stranded by utter destitution. Nor have all men had the same reasons for leaving their country and for seeking for a new one: some have escaped from their cities when destroyed by hostile armies, and having lost their own lands have been thrust upon those of others: some have been cast out by domestic quarrels: some have been driven forth in consequence of an excess of population, in order to relieve the pressure at home: some have been forced to leave by pestilence, or frequent earthquakes, or some unbearable defects of a barren soil: some have been seduced by the fame of a fertile and over-praised clime. Different people have been led away from their homes by different causes; but in all cases it is clear that nothing remains in the same place in which it was born: the movement of the human race is perpetual: in this vast world some changes take place daily. The foundations of new cities are laid, new names of nations arise, while the former ones die out, or become absorbed by more powerful ones. And yet what else are all these general migrations but the banishments of whole peoples? Why should I lead you through all these details? what is the use of mentioning Antenor the founder of Padua, or Evander who established his kingdom of Arcadian settlers on the banks of the Tiber? or Diomedes and the other heroes, both victors and vanquished, whom the Trojan war scattered over lands which were not their own? It is a fact that the Roman Empire itself traces its origin back to an exile as its founder, who, fleeing from his country after its conquest, with what few relics he had saved from the wreck, had been brought to Italy by hard necessity and fear of his conqueror, which bade him seek distant lands. Since then, how many colonies has this people sent forth into every province? wherever the Roman conquers, there he dwells. These migrations always found people eager to take part in them, and veteran soldiers desert their native hearths and follow the flag of the colonists across the sea. The matter does not need illustrations by any more examples: yet I will add one more which I have before my eyes: this very island has often changed its inhabitants. Not to mention more ancient events, which have become obscure from their antiquity, the Greeks who inhabit Marseilles at the present day, when they left Phocaea, first settled here, and it is doubtful what drove them hence, whether it was the rigour of the climate, the sight of the more powerful land of Italy, or the want of harbours on the coast: for the fact of their having placed themselves in the midst of what were then the most savage and uncouth tribes of Gaul proves that they were not driven hence by the ferocity of the natives. Subsequently the Ligurians came over into this same island, and also the Spaniards, which is proved by the resemblance of their customs: for they wear the same head-coverings and the same sort of shoes as the Cantabrians, and some of their words are the same: for by association with Greeks and Ligurians they have entirely lost their native speech. Hither since then have been brought two Roman colonies, one by Marius, the other by Sulla: so often has the population of this barren and thorny rock been changed. In fine, you will scarcely find any land which is still in the hands of its original inhabitants: all peoples have become confused and intermingled: one has come after another: one has wished for what another scorned: some have been driven out of the land which they took from another. Thus fate has decreed that nothing should ever enjoy an uninterrupted course of good fortune.

VIII. Varro, that most learned of all the Romans, thought that for the mere change of place, apart from the other evils attendant on exile, we may find a sufficient remedy in the thought that wherever we go we always have the same Nature to deal with. Marcus Brutus thought that there was sufficient comfort in the thought that those who go into exile are permitted to carry their virtues thither with them. Though one might think that neither of these alone were able to console an exile, yet it must be confessed that when combined they have great power: for how very little it is that we lose! whithersoever we betake ourselves two most excellent things will accompany us, namely, a common Nature and our own especial virtue. Believe me, this is the work of whoever was the Creator of the universe, whether he be an all-powerful deity, an incorporeal mind which effects vast works, a divine spirit by which all things from the greatest to the smallest are equally pervaded, or fate and an unalterable connected sequence of events, this, I say, is its work, that nothing above the very lowest can ever fall into the power of another: all that is best for a man's enjoyment lies beyond human power, and can neither be bestowed or taken away: this world, the greatest and the most beautiful of Nature's productions, and its noblest part, a mind which can behold and admire it, are our own property, and will remain with us as long as we ourselves endure. Let us therefore briskly and cheerfully hasten with undaunted steps whithersoever circumstances call us: let us wander over whatever countries we please; no place of banishment can be found in the whole world in which man cannot find a home. I can raise my eyes from the earth to the sky in one place as well as in another; the heavenly bodies are everywhere equally near to mankind: accordingly, as long as my eyes are not deprived of that spectacle of which they never can have their fill, as long as I am allowed to gaze on the sun and moon, to dwell upon the other stars, to speculate upon their risings and settings, their periods, and the reasons why they move faster or slower, to see so many stars glittering throughout the night, some fixed, some not moving in a wide orbit but revolving in their own proper track, some suddenly diverging from it, some dazzling our eyes by a fiery blaze as though they were falling, or flying along drawing after them a long trail of brilliant light: while I am permitted to commune with these, and to hold intercourse, as far as a human being may, with all the company of heaven, while I can raise my spirit aloft to view its kindred sparks above, what does it matter upon what soil I tread?

IX. "But this country does not produce beautiful or fruit-bearing trees; it is not watered by the courses of large or navigable rivers; it bears nothing which other nations would covet, since its produce barely suffices to support its inhabitants: no precious marbles are quarried here, no veins of gold and silver are dug out." What of that! It must be a narrow mind that takes pleasure in things of the earth: it ought to be turned away from them to the contemplation of those which can be seen everywhere, which are equally brilliant everywhere: we ought to reflect, also, that these vulgar matters by a mistaken perversion of ideas prevent really good things reaching us: the further men stretch out their porticos, the higher they raise their towers, the more widely they extend their streets, the deeper they sink their retreats from the heats of summer, the more ponderous the roofs with which they cover their banqueting halls, the more there will be to obstruct their view of heaven. Fortune has cast you into a country in which there is no lodging more splendid than a cottage: you must indeed have a poor spirit, and one which seeks low sources of consolation, if you endure this bravely because you have seen the cottage of Romulus: say, rather, "Should that lowly barn be entered by the virtues, it will straightway become more beautiful than any temple, because within it will be seen justice, self-restraint, prudence, love, a right division of all duties, a knowledge of all things on earth and in heaven. No place can be narrow, if it contains such a company of the greatest virtues; no exile can be irksome in which one can be attended by these companions. Brutus, in the book which he wrote upon virtue, says that he saw Marcellus in exile at Mytilene, living as happily as it is permitted to man to live, and never keener in his pursuit of literature than at that time. He consequently adds the reflexion: "I seemed rather to be going into exile myself when I had to return without him, than to be leaving him in exile." O how much more fortunate was Marcellus at that time, when Brutus praised him for his exile, than when Rome praised him for his consulship! what a man that must have been who made any one think himself exiled because he was leaving him in exile! what a man that must have been who attracted the admiration of one whom even his friend Cato admired! Brutus goes on to say:—"Gaius Caesar sailed past Mytilene without landing, because he could not bear to see a fallen man." The Senate did indeed obtain his recall by public petition, being so anxious and sorrowful the while, that you would have thought that they all were of Brutus's mind that day, and were not pleading the cause of Marcellus, but their own, that they might not be sent into exile by being deprived of him: yet he gained far greater glory on the day when Brutus could not bear to leave him in exile, and Caesar could not bear to see him: for each of them bore witness to his worth: Brutus grieved, and Caesar blushed at going home without Marcellus. Can you doubt that so great a man as Marcellus frequently encouraged himself to endure his exile patiently in some such terms as these: "The loss of your country is no misery to you: you have so steeped yourself in philosophic lore, as to know that all the world is the wise man's country? What! was not this very man who banished you absent from his country for ten successive years? he was, no doubt, engaged in the extension of the empire, but for all that he was absent from his country. Now see how his presence is required in Africa, which threatens to re-kindle the war, in Spain which is nursing up again the strength of the broken and shattered opposite faction, in treacherous Egypt, in fine, in all the parts of the world, for all are watching their opportunity to seize the empire at a disadvantage. Which will he go to meet first? which part of the universal conspiracy will he first oppose? His victory will drag him through every country in the world. Let nations look up to him and worship him: do thou live satisfied with the admiration of Brutus."

X. Marcellus, then, nobly endured his exile, and his change of place made no change in his mind, even though it was accompanied by poverty, in which every man who has not fallen into the madness of avarice and luxury, which upset all our ideas, sees no harm. Indeed, how very little is required to keep a man alive? and who, that has any virtue whatever, will find this fail him? As for myself, I do not feel that I have lost my wealth, but my occupation: the wants of the body are few: it wants protection from the cold, and the means of allaying hunger and thirst: all desires beyond these are vices, not necessities. There is no need for prying into all the depths of the sea, for loading one's stomach with heaps of slaughtered animals, or for tearing up shell-fish from the unknown shore of the furthest sea: may the gods and goddesses bring ruin upon those whose luxury transcends the bounds of an empire which is already perilously wide. They want to have their ostentatious kitchens supplied with game from the other side of the Phasis, and though Rome has not yet obtained satisfaction from the Parthians, they are not ashamed to obtain birds from them: they bring together from all regions everything, known or unknown, to tempt their fastidious palate: food, which their stomach, worn out with delicacies, can scarcely retain, is brought from the most distant ocean: they vomit that they may eat, and eat that they may vomit, and do not even deign to digest the banquets which they ransack the globe to obtain. If a man despises these things, what harm can poverty do him? If he desires them, then poverty even does him good, for he is cured in spite of himself, and though he will not receive remedies even upon compulsion, yet while he is unable to fulfil his wishes he is as though he had them not. Gaius Caesar, whom in my opinion Nature produced in order to show what unlimited vice would be capable of when combined with unlimited power, dined one day at a cost of ten millions of sesterces: and though in this he had the assistance of the intelligence of all his subjects, yet he could hardly find how to make one dinner out of the tribute-money of three provinces. How unhappy are they whose appetite can only be aroused by costly food! and the costliness of food depends not upon its delightful flavour and sweetness of taste, but upon its rarity and the difficulty of procuring it: otherwise, if they chose to return to their sound senses, what need would they have of so many arts which minister to the stomach? of so great a commerce? of such ravaging of forests? of such ransacking of the depths of the sea? Food is to be found everywhere, and has been placed by Nature in every part the world, but they pass it by as though they were blind, and wander through all countries, cross the seas, and excite at a great cost the hunger which they might allay at a small one. One would like to say: Why do you launch ships? why do you arm your hands for battle both with men and wild beasts? why do you run so riotously hither and thither? why do you amass fortune after fortune? Are you unwilling to remember how small our bodies are?

is it not frenzy and the wildest insanity to wish for so much when you can contain so little? Though you may increase your income, and extend the boundaries of your property, yet you never can enlarge your own bodies: when your business transactions have turned out well, when you have made a successful campaign, when you have collected the food for which you have hunted through all lands, you will have no place in which to bestow all these superfluities. Why do you strive to obtain so much? Do you think that our ancestors, whose virtue supports our vices even to the present day, were unhappy, though they dressed their food with their own hands, though the earth was their bed, though their roofs did not yet glitter with gold, nor their temples with precious stones? and so they used then to swear with scrupulous honesty by earthenware gods; those who called these gods to witness would go back to the enemy for certain death rather than break their word. Do you suppose that our dictator who granted an audience to the ambassadors of the Samnites, while he roasted the commonest food before the fire himself with that very hand with which he had so often smitten the enemy, and with which he had placed his laurel wreath upon the lap of Capitolian Jove, enjoyed life less than the Apicius who lived in our own days, whose habits tainted the entire century, who set himself up as a professor of gastronomy in that very city from which philosophers once were banished as corruptors of youth? It is worth while to know his end. After he had spent a hundred millions of sesterces on his kitchen, and had wasted on each single banquet a sum equal to so many presents from the reigning emperors, and the vast revenue which he drew from the Capitol, being overburdened with debt, he then for the first time was forced to examine his accounts: he calculated that he would have ten millions left of his fortune, and, as though he would live a life of mere starvation on ten millions, put an end to his life by poison. How great must the luxury of that man have been, to whom ten millions signified want? Can you think after this that the amount of money necessary to make a fortune depends upon its actual extent rather than on the mind of the owner? Here was a man who shuddered at the thought of a fortune of ten million sesterces, and escaped by poison from a prospect which other men pray for. Yet, for a mind so diseased, that last draught of his was the most wholesome: he was really eating and drinking poisons when he was not only enjoying, but boasting of his enormous banquets, when he was flaunting his vices, when he was causing his country to follow his example, when he was inviting youths to imitate him, albeit youth is quick to learn evil, without being provided with a model to copy. This is what befalls those who do not use their wealth according to reason, which has fixed limits, but according to vicious fashion, whose caprices are boundless and immeasurable. Nothing is sufficient for covetous desire, but Nature can be satisfied even with scant measure. The poverty of an exile, therefore, causes no inconvenience, for no place of exile is so barren as not to produce what is abundantly sufficient to support a man.

XI. Next, need an exile regret his former dress and house? If he only wishes for these things because of their use to him, he will want neither roof nor garment, for it takes as little to cover the body as it does to feed it: Nature has annexed no difficult conditions to anything which man is obliged to do. If, however, he sighs for a purple robe steeped in floods of dye, interwoven with threads of gold and with many coloured artistic embroideries, then his poverty is his own fault, not that of Fortune: even though you restored to him all that he has lost, you would do him no good; for he would have more unsatisfied ambitions, if restored, than he had unsatisfied wants when he was an exile. If he longs for furniture glittering with silver vases, plate which boasts the signature of antique artists, bronze which the mania of a small clique has rendered costly, slaves enough to crowd however large a house, purposely overfed horses, and precious stones of all countries: whatever collections he may make of these, he never will satisfy his insatiable appetite, any more than any amount of liquor will quench a thirst which arises not from the need of drink but from the burning heat within a man; for this is not thirst but disease. Nor does this take place only with regard to money and food, but every want which is caused by vice and not by necessity is of this nature: however much you supply it with you do not quench it but intensify it. He who restrains himself within the limits prescribed by nature, will not feel poverty; he who exceeds them will always be poor, however great his wealth may be. Even a place of exile suffices to provide one with necessaries; whole kingdoms do not suffice to provide one with superfluities. It is the mind which makes men rich: this it is that accompanies them into exile, and in the most savage wildernesses, after having found sufficient sustenance for the body, enjoys its own overflowing resources: the mind has no more connexion with money than the immortal gods have with those things which are so highly valued by untutored intellects, sunk in the bondage of the flesh. Gems, gold, silver, and vast polished round tables are but earthly dross, which cannot be loved by a pure mind that is mindful of whence it came, is unblemished by sin, and which, when released from the body, will straightway soar aloft to the highest heaven: meanwhile, as far as it is permitted by the hindrances of its mortal limbs and this heavy clog of the body by which it is surrounded, it examines divine things with swift and airy thought. From this it follows that no free-born man, who is akin to the gods, and fit for any world and any age, can ever be in exile: for his thoughts are directed to all the heavens and to all times past and future: this trumpery body, the prison and fetter of the spirit, may be tossed to this place or to that; upon it tortures, robberies, and diseases may work their will: but the spirit itself is holy and eternal, and upon it no one can lay hands.

XII. That you may not suppose that I merely use the maxims of the philosophers to disparage the evils of poverty, which no one finds terrible, unless he thinks it so; consider in the first place how many more poor people there are than rich, and yet you will not find that they are sadder or more anxious than the rich: nay, I am not sure that they are not happier, because they have fewer things to distract their minds. From these poor men, who often are not unhappy at their poverty, let us pass to the rich. How many occasions there are on which they are just like poor men! When they are on a journey their baggage is cut down, whenever they are obliged to travel fast their train of attendants is dismissed. When they are serving in the army, how small a part of their property can they have with them, since camp discipline forbids superfluities! Nor is it only temporary exigences or desert places that put them on the same level as poor men: they have some days on which they become sick of their riches, dine reclining on the ground, put away all their gold and silver plate, and use earthenware. Madmen! they are always afraid of this for which they sometimes wish. O how dense a stupidity, how great an ignorance of the truth they show when they flee from this thing and yet amuse themselves by playing with it! Whenever I look back to the great examples of antiquity, I feel ashamed to seek consolation for my poverty, now that luxury has advanced so far in the present age, that the allowance of an exile is larger than the inheritance of the princes of old. It is well known that Homer had one slave, that Plato had three, and that Zeno, who first taught the stern and masculine doctrine of the Stoics, had none: yet could any one say that they lived wretchedly without himself being thought a most pitiable wretch by all men? Menenius Agrippa, by whose mediation the patricians and plebeians were reconciled, was buried by public subscription. Attilius Regulus, while he was engaged in scattering the Carthaginians in Africa, wrote to the Senate that his hired servant had left him, and that consequently his farm was deserted: whereupon it was decreed that as long as Regulus was absent, it should be cultivated at the expense of the state. Was it not worth his while to have no slave, if thereby he obtained the Roman people for his farm-bailiff? Scipio's daughters received their dowries from the Treasury, because their father had left them none: by Hercules, it was right for the Roman people to pay tribute to Scipio for once, since he had exacted it for ever from Carthage. O how happy were those girls' husbands, who had the Roman people for their father-in-law. Can you think that those whose daughters dance in the ballet, and marry with a settlement of a million sesterces, are happier than Scipio, whose children received their dowry of old-fashioned brass money from their guardian the Senate? Can any one despise poverty, when she has such a noble descent to boast of? can an exile be angry at any privation, when Scipio could not afford a portion for his daughters, Regulus could not afford a hired labourer, Menenius could not afford a funeral? when all these men's wants were supplied in a manner which rendered them a source of additional honour? Poverty, when such men as these plead its cause, is not only harmless, but positively attractive.

XIII. To this one may answer: "Why do you thus ingeniously divide what can indeed be endured if taken singly, but which all together are overwhelming? Change of place can be borne if nothing more than one's place be changed: poverty can be borne if it be without disgrace, which is enough to cow our spirits by itself." If any one were to endeavour to frighten me with the number of my misfortunes, I should answer him as follows: If you have enough strength to resist any one part of your ill-fortune, you will have enough to resist it all. If virtue has once hardened your mind, it renders it impervious to blows from any quarter: if avarice, that greatest pest of the human race, has left it, you will not be troubled by ambition: if you regard the end of your days not as a punishment, but as an ordinance of nature, no fear of anything else will dare to enter the breast which has cast out the fear of death. If you consider sexual passion to have been bestowed on mankind not for the sake of pleasure, but for the continuance of the race, all other desires will pass harmlessly by one who is safe even from this secret plague, implanted in our very bosoms. Reason does not conquer vices one by one, but all together: if reason is defeated, it is utterly defeated once for all. Do you suppose that any wise man, who relies entirely upon himself, who has set himself free from the ideas of the common herd, can be wrought upon by disgrace? A disgraceful death is worse even than disgrace: yet Socrates bore the same expression of countenance with which he had rebuked thirty tyrants, when he entered the prison and thereby took away the infamous character of the place; for the place which contained Socrates could not be regarded as a prison. Was any one ever so blind to the truth as to suppose that Marcus Cato was disgraced by his double defeat in his candidature for the praetorship and the consulship? that disgrace fell on the praetorship and consulship which Cato honoured by his candidature. No one is despised by others unless he be previously despised by himself: a grovelling and abject mind may fall an easy prey to such contempt: but he who stands up against the most cruel misfortunes, and overcomes those evils by which others would have been crushed—such a man, I say, turns his misfortunes into badges of honour, because we are so constituted as to admire nothing so much as a man who bears adversity bravely. At Athens, when Aristides was being led to execution, every one who met him cast down his eyes and groaned, as though not merely a just man but justice herself was being put to death. Yet one man was found who spat in his face: he might have been disturbed at this, since he knew it could only be a foul-mouthed fellow that would have the heart to do so; he, however, wiped his face, and with a smile asked the magistrate who accompanied him to warn that man not to open his mouth so rudely again. To act thus was to treat contumely itself with contempt. I know that some say that there is nothing more terrible than disgrace, and that they would prefer death. To such men I answer that even exile is often accompanied by no disgrace whatever: if a great man falls, he remains a great man after his fall, you can no more suppose that he is disgraced than when people tread upon the walls of a ruined temple, which the pious treat with as much respect as when they were standing.

XIV. Since, then, my dearest mother, you have no reason for endless weeping on my account, it follows that your tears must flow on your own: there are two causes for this, either your having lost my protection, or your not being able to bear the mere fact of separation. The first of these I shall only touch upon lightly, for I know that your heart loves nothing belonging to your children except themselves. Let other mothers look to that, who make use of their sons' authority with a woman's passion, who are ambitious through their sons because they cannot bear office themselves, who spend their sons' inheritance, and yet are eager to inherit it, and who weary their sons by lending their eloquence to others: you have always rejoiced exceedingly in the successes of your sons, and have made no use of them whatever: you have always set bounds to our generosity, although you set none to your own: you, while a minor under the power of the head of the family, still used to make presents to your wealthy sons: you managed our inheritances with as much care as if you were working for your own, yet refrained from touching them as scrupulously as if they belonged to strangers: you have spared to use our influence, as though you enjoyed other means of your own, and you have taken no part in the public offices to which we have been elected beyond rejoicing in our success and paying our expenses: your indulgence has never been tainted by any thought of profit, and you cannot regret the loss of your son for a reason which never had any weight with you before his exile.

XV. All my powers of consolation must be directed to the other point, the true source of your maternal grief. You say, "I am deprived of the embraces of my darling son, I cannot enjoy the pleasure of seeing him and of hearing him talk. Where is he at whose sight I used to smooth my troubled brow, in whose keeping I used to deposit all my cares? Where is his conversation, of which I never could have enough? his studies, in which I used to take part with more than a woman's eagerness, with more than a mother's familiarity? Where are our meetings? the boyish delight which he always showed at the sight of his mother?" To all this you add the actual places of our merrymakings and conversation, and, what must needs have more power to move you than anything else, the traces of our late social life, for Fortune treated you with the additional cruelty of allowing you to depart on the very third day before my ruin, without a trace of anxiety, and not fearing anything of the kind. It was well that we had been separated by a vast distance: it was well that an absence of some years had prepared you to bear this blow: you came home, not to take any pleasure in your son, but to get rid of the habit of longing for him. Had you been absent long before, you would have borne it more bravely, as the very length of your absence would have moderated your longing to see me: had you never gone away, you would at any rate have gained one last advantage in seeing your son for two days longer: as it was, cruel Fate so arranged it that you were not present with me during my good fortune, and yet have not become accustomed to my absence. But the harder these things are to bear, the more virtue you must summon to your aid, and the more bravely you must struggle as it were with an enemy whom you know well, and whom you have already often conquered. This blood did not flow from a body previously unhurt: you have been struck through the scar of an old wound.

XVI. You have no grounds for excusing yourself on the ground of being a woman, who has a sort of right to weep without restraint, though not without limit. For this reason our ancestors allotted a space of ten months' mourning for women who had lost their husbands, thus settling the violence of a woman's grief by a public ordinance. They did not forbid them to mourn, but they set limits to their grief: for while it is a foolish weakness to give way to endless grief when you lose one of those dearest to you, yet it shows an unnatural hardness of heart to express no grief at all: the best middle course between affection and hard common sense is both to feel regret and to restrain it. You need not look at certain women whose sorrow, when once begun, has been ended only by death: you know some who after the loss of their sons have never laid aside the garb of mourning: you are constitutionally stronger than these, and from you more is required. You cannot avail yourself of the excuse of being a woman, for you have no womanish vices. Unchastity, the greatest evil of the age, has never classed you with the majority of women; you have not been tempted either by gems or by pearls; riches have not allured you into thinking them the greatest blessing that man can own; respectably brought up as you were in an old-fashioned and strict household, you have never been led astray by that imitation of others which is so full of danger even to virtuous women. You have never been ashamed of your fruitfulness as though it were a reproach to your youth: you never concealed the signs of pregnancy as though it were an unbecoming burden, nor did you ever destroy your expected child within your womb after the fashion of many other women, whose attractions are to be found in their beauty alone. You never defiled your face with paints or cosmetics: you never liked clothes which showed the figure as plainly as though it were naked: your sole ornament has been a consummate loveliness which no time can impair, your greatest glory has been your modesty. You cannot, therefore, plead your womanhood as an excuse for your grief, because your virtues have raised you above it: you ought to be as superior to womanish tears as you are to womanish vices. Even women would not allow you to pine away after receiving this blow, but would bid you quickly and calmly go through the necessary amount of mourning, and then to arise and shake it off: I mean, if you are willing to take as your models those women whose eminent virtue has given them a place among even great men. Misfortune reduced the number of Cornelia's children from twelve to two: if you count the number of their deaths, Cornelia had lost ten: if you weigh them, she had lost the Gracchi: nevertheless, when her friends were weeping around her and using too bitter imprecations against her fate, she forbade them to blame fortune for having deprived her of her sons the Gracchi. Such ought to have been the mother of him who, when speaking in the Forum, said, "Would you speak evil of the mother who bore me?" The mother's speech seems to me to show a far greater spirit: the son set a high value on the birth of the Gracchi; the mother set an equal value on their deaths. Rutilia followed her son Cotta into exile, and was so passionately attached to him that she could bear exile better than absence from him;

nor did she return home before her son did so: after he had been restored, and had been raised to honour in the republic, she bore his death as bravely as she had borne his exile. No one saw any traces of tears upon her cheeks after she had buried her son: she displayed her courage when he was banished, her wisdom when he died: she allowed no considerations either to interfere with her affection, or to force her to protract a useless and foolish mourning. These are the women with whom I wish you to be numbered: you have the best reasons for restraining and suppressing your sorrow as they did, because you have always imitated their lives.

XVII. I am aware that this is a matter which is not in our power, and that none of the passions, least of all that which arises from grief, are obedient to our wishes; indeed, it is overbearing and obstinate, and stubbornly rejects all remedies: we sometimes wish to crush it, and to swallow our emotion, but, nevertheless, tears flow over our carefully arranged and made-up countenance. Sometimes we occupy our minds with public spectacles and shows of gladiators; but during the very sights by which it is amused, the mind is wrung by slight touches of sorrow. It is better, therefore, to conquer it than to cheat it; for a grief which has been deceived and driven away either by pleasure or by business rises again, and its period of rest does but give it strength for a more terrible attack; but a grief which has been conquered by reason is appeased for ever. I shall not, then, give you the advice which so many, I know, adopt, that you should distract your thoughts by a long journey, or amuse them by a beautiful one; that you should spend much of your time in the careful examination of accounts, and the management of your estate, and that you should keep constantly engaging in new enterprises: all these things avail but little, and do not cure, but merely obstruct our sorrow. I had rather it should be brought to an end than that it should be cheated: and, therefore, I would fain lead you to the study of philosophy, the true place of refuge for all those who are flying from the cruelty of Fortune: this will heal your wounds and take away all your sadness: to this you would now have to apply yourself, even though you had never done so before; but as far as my father's old-fashioned strictness permitted, you have gained a superficial, though not a thorough knowledge of all liberal studies. Would that my father, most excellent man that he was, had been less devoted to the customs of our ancestors, and had been willing to have you thoroughly instructed in the elements of philosophy, instead of receiving a mere smattering of it! I should not now need to be providing you with the means of struggling against Fortune, but you would offer them to me: but he did not allow you to pursue your studies far, because some women use literature to teach them luxury instead of wisdom. Still, thanks to your keen intellectual appetite, you learned more than one could have expected in the time: you laid the foundations of all good learning: now return to them: they will render you safe, they will console you, and charm you. If once they have thoroughly entered into your mind, grief, anxiety, the distress of vain suffering will never gain admittance thither: your breast will not be open to any of these; against all other vices it has long been closed. Philosophy is your most trustworthy guardian, and it alone can save you from the attacks of Fortune.

XVIII. Since, however, you require something to lean upon until you can reach that haven of rest which philosophy offers to you, I wish in the meantime to point out to you the consolations which you have. Look at my two brothers—while they are safe, you have no grounds for complaint against Fortune; you can derive pleasure from the virtues of each of them, different as they are; the one has gained high office by attention to business, the other has philosophically despised it. Rejoice in the great place of one of your sons, in the peaceful retirement of the other, in the filial affection of both. I know my brothers' most secret motives: the one adorns his high office in order to confer lustre upon you, the other has withdrawn from the world into his life of quiet and contemplation, that he may have full enjoyment of your society. Fortune has consulted both your safety and your pleasure in her disposal of your two sons: you may be protected by the authority of the one, and delighted by the literary leisure of the other. They will vie with one another in dutiful affection to you, and the loss of one son will be supplied by the love of two others. I can confidently promise that you will find nothing wanting in your sons except their number. Now, then, turn your eyes from them to your grandchildren; to Marcus, that most engaging child, whose sight no sorrow can withstand. No grief can be so great or so fresh in any one's bosom as not to be charmed away by his presence. Where are the tears which his joyousness could not dry? whose heart is so nipped by sorrow that his animation would not cause it to dilate? who would not be rendered mirthful by his playfulness? who would not be attracted and made to forget his gloomy thoughts by that prattle to which no one can ever be weary of listening? I pray the gods that be may survive us: may all the cruelty of fate exhaust itself on me and go no further; may all the sorrow destined for my mother and my grandmother fall upon me; but let all the rest flourish as they do now: I shall make no complaints about my childlessness or my exile, if only my sacrifice may be received as a sufficient atonement, and my family suffer nothing more. Hold in your bosom Novatilla, who soon will present you with great-grandchildren, she whom I had so entirely adopted and made my own, that, now that she has lost me, she seems like an orphan, even though her father is alive. Love her for my sake as well as for her own: Fortune has lately deprived her of her mother: your affection will be able to prevent her really feeling the loss of the mother whom she mourns. Take this opportunity of forming and strengthening her principles; nothing sinks so deeply into the mind as the teaching which we receive in our earliest years; let her become accustomed to hearing your discourses; let her character be moulded according to your pleasure: she will gain much even if you give her nothing more than your example. This continually recurring duty will be a remedy in itself: for when your mind is full of maternal sorrow, nothing can distract it from its grief except either philosophic argument or honourable work. I should count your father among your greatest consolations, were he not absent: as it is, judge from your affection for me what his affection is for you, and then you will see how much more just it is that you should be preserved for him than that you should be sacrificed to me. Whenever your keenest paroxysms of grief assail you and bid you give way to them, think of your father. By giving him so many grandchildren and great-grandchildren you have made yourself no longer his only daughter; but you alone can crown his prosperous life by a happy end: as long as he is alive it is impiety for you to regret having been born.

XIX. I have hitherto said nothing of your chief source of consolation, your sister, that most faithful heart which shares all your sorrows as fully as your own, and who feels for all of us like a mother. With her you have mingled your tears, on her bosom you have tasted your first repose: she always feels for your troubles, and when I am in the case she does not grieve for you alone. It was in her arms that I was carried into Rome: by her affectionate and motherly nursing I regained my strength after a long period of sickness: she enlarged her influence to obtain the office of quaestor for me, and her fondness for me made her conquer a shyness which at other times made her shrink from speaking to, or loudly greeting her friends. Neither her retired mode of life, nor her country-bred modesty, at a time when so many women display such boldness of manner, her placidity, nor her habits of solitary seclusion prevented her from becoming actually ambitious on my account. Here, my dearest mother, is a source from which you may gain true consolation: join yourself, as far as you are able, to her, bind yourself to her by the closest embraces. Those who are in sorrow are wont to flee from those who are dearest to them, and to seek liberty for the indulgence of their grief: do you let her share your every thought: if you wish to nurse your grief, she will be your companion, if you wish to lay it aside she will bring it to an end.

If, however, I rightly understand the wisdom of that most perfect woman, she will not suffer you to waste your life in unprofitable mourning, and will tell you what happened in her own instance, which I myself witnessed. During a sea-voyage she lost a beloved husband, my uncle, whom she married when a maiden; she endured at the same time grief for him and fear for herself, and at last, though shipwrecked, nevertheless rescued his body from the vanquished tempest. How many noble deeds are unknown to fame! If only she had had the simple-minded ancients to admire her virtues, how many brilliant intellects would have vied with one another in singing the praises of a wife who forgot the weakness of her sex, forgot the perils of the sea, which terrify even the boldest, exposed herself to death in order to lay him in the earth, and who was so eager to give him decent burial that she cared nothing about whether she shared it or no. All the poets have made the wife famous who gave herself to death instead of her husband: my aunt did more when she risked her life in order to give her husband a tomb: it shows greater love to endure the same peril for a less important end. After this, no one need wonder that for sixteen years, during which her husband governed the province of Egypt, she was never beheld in public, never admitted any of the natives to her house, never begged any favour of her husband, and never allowed anyone to beg one of her. Thus it came to pass that a gossiping province, ingenious in inventing scandal about its rulers, in which even the blameless often incurred disgrace, respected her as a singular example of uprightness, never made free with her name,—a remarkable piece of self-restraint among a people who will risk everything rather than forego a jest,—and that at the present time it hopes for another governor's wife like her, although it has no reasonable expectation of ever seeing one. It would have been greatly to her credit if the province had approved her conduct for a space of sixteen years: it was much more creditable to her that it knew not of her existence. I do not remind you of this in order to celebrate her praises, for to take such scanty notice of them is to curtail them, but in order that you may understand the magnanimity of a woman who has not yielded either to ambition or to avarice, those twin attendants and scourges of authority, who, when her ship was disabled and her own death was impending, was not restrained by fear from keeping fast hold of her husband's dead body, and who sought not how to escape from the wreck, but how to carry him out of it with her. You must now show a virtue equal to hers, recall your mind from grief, and take care that no one may think that you are sorry that you have borne a son.

XX. However, since it is necessary, whatever you do, that your thoughts should sometimes revert to me, and that I should now be present to your mind more often than your other children, not because they are less dear to you, but because it is natural to lay one's hands more often upon a place that pains one; learn how you are to think of me: I am as joyous and cheerful as in my best days: indeed these days are my best, because my mind is relieved from all pressure of business and is at leisure to attend to its own affairs, and at one time amuses itself with lighter studies, at another eagerly presses its inquiries into its own nature and that of the universe: first it considers the countries of the world and their position: then the character of the sea which flows between them, and the alternate ebbings and flowings of its tides; next it investigates all the terrors which hang between heaven and earth, the region which is torn asunder by thunderings, lightnings, gusts of wind, vapour, showers of snow and hail. Finally, having traversed every one of the realms below, it soars to the highest heaven, enjoys the noblest of all spectacles, that of things divine, and, remembering itself to be eternal, reviews all that has been and all that will be for ever and ever.

ROBERT LOUIS STEVENSON

On the Enjoyment of Unpleasant Places

It is a difficult matter to make the most of any given place, and we have much in our own power. Things looked at patiently from one side after another generally end by showing a side that is beautiful. A few months ago some words were said in the *Portfolio* as to an "austere regimen in scenery"; and such a discipline was then recommended as "healthful and strengthening to the taste." That is the text, so to speak, of the present essay. This discipline in scenery, it must be understood, is something more than a mere walk before breakfast to whet the appetite. For when we are put down in some unsightly neighborhood, and especially if we have come to be more or less dependent on what we see, we must set ourselves to hunt out beautiful things with all the ardour and patience of a botanist after a rare plant. Day by day we perfect ourselves in the art of seeing nature more favourably. We learn to live with her, as people learn to live with fretful or violent spouses: to dwell lovingly on what is good, and shut our eyes against all that is bleak or inharmonious. We learn, also, to come to each place in the right spirit. The traveller, as Brantôme quaintly tells us, "*fait des discours en soi pour se soutenir en chemin*"; and into these discourses he weaves something out of all that he sees and suffers by the way; they take their tone greatly from the varying character of the scene; a sharp ascent brings different thoughts from a level road; and the man's fancies grow lighter as he comes out of the wood into a clearing. Nor does the scenery any more affect the thoughts than the thoughts affect the seenery. We see places through our humours as through differently colored glasses. We are ourselves a term in the equation, a note of the chord, and make discord or harmony almost at will. There is no fear for the result, if we can but surrender ourselves sufficiently to the country that surrounds and follows us, so that we are ever thinking suitable thoughts or telling ourselves some suitable sort of story as we go. We become thus, in some sense, a centre of beauty; we are provocative of beauty, much as a gentle and sincere character is provocative of sincerity and gentleness in others. And even where there is no harmony to be elicited by the quickest and most obedient of spirits, we may still embellish a place with some attraction of romance. We may learn to go far afield for associations, and handle them lightly when we have found them. Sometimes an old print comes to our aid; I have seen many a spot lit up at once with picturesque imaginations, by a reminiscence of Callot, or Sadeler, or Paul Brill. Dick Turpin has been my lay figure for many an English lane. And I suppose the Trossachs would hardly be the Trossachs for most tourists if a man of admirable romantic instinct had not peopled it for them with harmonious figures, and brought them thither their minds rightly prepared for the impression. There is half the battle in this preparation. For instance: I have rarely been able to visit, in the proper spirit, the wild and inhospitable places of our own Highlands. I am happier where it is tame and fertile, and not readily pleased without trees. I understand that there are some phases of mental trouble that harmonise well with such surroundings, and that some persons, by the dispensing power of the imagination, can go back several centuries in spirit, and put themselves into sympathy with the hunted, houseless, unsociable way of life that was in its place upon these savage hills. Now, when I am sad, I like nature to charm me out of my sadness, like David before Saul; and the thought of these past ages strikes nothing in me but an unpleasant pity; so that I can never hit on the right humour for this sort of landscape, and lose much pleasure in consequence. Still, even here, if I were only let alone, and time enough were given, I should have all manner of pleasure, and take many clear and beautiful images away with me when I left. When we cannot think ourselves into sympathy with the great features of a country, we learn to ignore them, and put our head among the grass for flowers, or pore, for long times together, over the changeful current of a stream. We come down to the sermon in stones, when we are shut out from any poem in the spread landscape. We begin to peep and botanise, we take an interest in birds and insects, we find many things beautiful in miniature. The reader will recollect the little summer scene in *Wuthering Heights*—the one warm scene, perhaps, in all that powerful, miserable novel—and the great feature that is made therein by grasses and flowers and a little sunshine: this is in the spirit of which I now speak. And, lastly, we can go indoors; interiors are sometimes as beautiful, often more picturesque, than the shows of the open air, and they have that quality of shelter of which I shall presently have more to say.

With all this in mind, I have often been tempted to put forth the paradox that any place is good enough to live a life in, while it is only in a few, and those highly favoured, that we can pass a few hours agreeably. For, if we only stay long enough, we become at home in the neighbourhood. Reminiscences spring up, like flowers, about uninteresting corners. We forget to some degree the superior loveliness of other places, and fall into a tolerant and sympathetic spirit which is its own reward and justification. Looking back the other day on some recollections of my own, I was astonished to find how much I owed to such a residence; six weeks in one unpleasant countryside had done more, it seemed, to quicken and educate my sensibilities than many years in places that jumped more nearly with my inclination.

The country to which I refer was a level and treeless plateau, over which the winds cut like a whip. For miles on miles it was the same. A river, indeed, fell into the sea near the town where I resided; but the valley of the river was shallow and bald, for as far up as ever I had the heart to follow it. There were roads, certainly, but roads that had no beauty or interest; for, as there was no timber, and but little irregularity of surface, you saw your whole walk exposed to you from the beginning: there was nothing left to fancy, nothing to expect, nothing to see by the wayside, save here and there an unhomely-looking homestead, and here and there a solitary, spectacled stone-breaker; and you were only accompanied, as you went doggedly forward by the gaunt telegraph-posts and the hum of the resonant wires in the keen sea-wind. To one who has learned to know their song in warm pleasant places by the Mediterranean, it seemed to taunt the country, and make it still bleaker by suggested contrast. Even the waste places by the side of the road were not, as Hawthorne liked to put it, "taken back to Nature" by any decent covering of vegetation. Wherever the land had the chance, it seemed to lie fallow. There is a certain tawny nudity of the South, bare sunburnt plains, coloured like a lion, and hills clothed only in the blue transparent air; but this was of another description—this was the nakedness of the North; the earth seemed to know that it was naked, and was ashamed and cold.

It seemed to be always blowing on that coast. Indeed, this had passed into the speech of the inhabitants, and they saluted each other when they met with "Breezy, breezy," instead of the customary "Fine day" of farther south. These continual winds were not like the harvest breeze, that just keeps an equable pressure against your face as you walk, and serves to set all the trees talking over your head, or bring round you the smell of the wet surface of the country after a shower. They were of the bitter, hard, persistent sort, that interferes with sight and respiration, and makes the eyes sore. Even such winds as these have their own merit in proper time and place. It is pleasant to see them brandish great masses of shadow. And what a power they have over the colour of the world! How they ruffle the solid woodlands in their passage, and make them shudder and whiten like a single willow! There is nothing more vertiginous than a wind like this among the woods, with all its sights and noises; and the effect gets between some painters and their sober eyesight, so that, even when the rest of their picture is calm, the foliage is coloured like foliage in a gale. There was nothing, however, of this sort to be noticed in a country where there were no trees and hardly any shadows, save the passive shadows and clouds or those of rigid houses and walls. But the wind was nevertheless an occasion of pleasure; for nowhere could you taste more fully the pleasure of a sudden lull, or a place of opportune shelter. The reader knows what I mean; he must remember how, when he has sat himself down behind a dyke on a hill-side, he delighted to hear the wind hiss vainly through the crannies at his back; how his body tingled all over with warmth, and it began to dawn upon him, with a sort of slow surprise, that the country was beautiful, the heather purple, and the faraway hills all marbled with sun and shadow. Wordsworth, in a beautiful passage of the "Prelude," has used this as a figure for the feeling struck in us by the quiet by-streets of London after the uproar of the great thoroughfares; and the comparison may be turned the other way with as good effect:

"Meanwhile the roar continues, till at
    length,
Escaped as from an enemy we turn,
Abruptly into some sequester'd nook,
Still as a shelter'd place when winds
    blow loud!"

I remember meeting a man once, in a train, who told me of what must have been quite the most perfect instance of this pleasure of escape.

He had gone up, one sunny, windy morning, to the top of a great cathedral somewhere abroad; I think it was Cologne Cathedral, the great unfinished marvel by the Rhine; and after a long while in dark stairways, he issued at last into the sunshine, on a platform high above the town. At that elevation it was quite still and warm; the gale was only in the lower strata of the air, and he had forgotten it in the quiet interior of the church and during his long ascent; and so you may judge of his surprise when, resting his arms on the sunlit balustrade and looking over into the *Place* far below him, he saw the good people holding on their hats and leaning hard against the wind as they walked. There is something, to my fancy, quite perfect in this little experience of my fellow-traveller's. The ways of men seem always very trivial to us when we find ourselves alone on a church-top, with the blue sky and a few tall pinnacles, and see far below us the steep roofs and foreshortened buttresses, and the silent activity of the city streets; but how much more must they not have seemed so to him as he stood, not only above other men's business, but above other men's climate, in a golden zone like Apollo's!

This was the sort of pleasure I found in the country of which I write. The pleasure was to be out of the wind, and to keep it in memory all the time, and hug oneself upon the shelter. And it was only by the sea that any such sheltered places were to be found. Between the black worm-eaten headlands there are little bights and havens, well screened from the wind and the commotion of the external sea, where the sand and weeds look up into the gazer's face from a depth of tranquil water, and the seabirds, screaming and flickering from the ruined crags, alone disturb the silence and the sunshine. One such place has impressed itself on my memory beyond all others. On a rock by the water's edge, old fighting men of the Norse breed had planted a double castle; the two stood wall to wall like semidetached villas; and yet feud had run so high between their owners, that one, from out of a window, shot the other as he stood in his own doorway. There is something in the juxtaposition of these two enemies full of tragic irony. It is grim to think of bearded men and bitter women taking hateful counsel together about the two hall-fires at night, when the sea boomed against the foundations and the wild winter wind was loose over the battlements. And in the study we may reconstruct for ourselves some pale figure of what life then was. Not so when we are there; when we are there such thoughts come to us only to intensify a contrary impression, and association is turned against itself. I remember walking thither three after-noons in succession, my eyes weary with being set against the wind, and how, dropping suddenly over the edge of the down, I found myself in a new world of warmth and shelter. The wind, from which I had escaped, "as from an enemy," was seemingly quite local. It carried no clouds with it, and came from such a quarter that it did not trouble the sea within view. The two castles, black and ruinous as the rocks about them, were still distinguishable from these by something more insecure and fantastic in the outline, something that the last storm had left imminent and the next would demolish entirely. It would be diffi-cult to render in words the sense of peace that took possession of me on these three afternoons. It was helped out, as I have said, by the con-trast. The shore was battered and bemauled by previous tempests; I had the memory at heart of the insane strife of the pigmies who had erected these two castles and lived in them in mutual dis-trust and enmity, and knew I had only to put my head out of this little cup of shelter to find the hard wind blowing in my eyes; and yet there were the two great tracts of motionless blue air and peaceful sea looking on, unconcerned and apart, at the turmoil of the present moment and the memorials of the precarious past. There is ever something transitory and fretful in the impression of a high wind under a cloudless sky; it seems to have no root in the constitution of things; it must speedily begin to faint and wither away like a cut flower. And on those days the thought of the wind and the thought of human life came very near together in my mind. Our noisy years did indeed seem moments in the being of the eternal silence: and the wind, in the face of that great field of stationary blue, was as the wind of a butterfly's wing. The placidity of the sea was a thing likewise to be remembered. Shelley speaks of the sea as "hungering for calm," and in this place one learned to understand the phrase. Looking down into these green waters from the broken edge of the rock, or swimming leisurely in the sunshine, it seemed to me that they were enjoying their own tranquillity; and when now and again it was disturbed by a wind ripple on the surface, or the quick black passage of a fish far below, they settled back again (one could fancy) with relief.

On shore, too, in the little nook of shelter, everything was so subdued and still that the least particular struck in me a pleasurable surprise.

The desultory crackling of the whin-pods in the afternoon sun usurped the ear. The hot, sweet breath of the bank, that had been saturated all day long with sunshine, and now exhaled it into my face, was like the breath of a fellow-creature. I remember that I was haunted by two lines of French verse; in some dumb way they seemed to fit my surroundings and give expression to the contentment that was in me, and I kept repeating to myself—

"Mon cœur est un luth suspendu,
Sitôt qu'on le touche, il résonne."

I can give no reason why these lines came to me at this time; and for that very cause I repeat them here. For all I know, they may serve to complete the impression in the mind of the reader, as they were certainly a part of it for me.

And this happened to me in the place of all others where I liked least to stay. When I think of it I grew ashamed of my own ingratitude. "Out of the strong came forth sweetness." There, in the bleak and gusty North, I received, perhaps, my strongest impression of peace. I saw the sea to be great and calm; and the earth, in that little corner, was all alive and friendly to me.

So, wherever a man is, he will find something to please and pacify him: in the town he will meet pleasant faces of men and women, and see beautiful flowers at a window, or hear cage-bird singing at the corner of the gloomiest street; and for the country, there is no country without some amenity—let him only look for it in the right spirit, and he will surely find.

GERTRUDE BELL

Travelling Companions

All the earth is seamed with roads, and all the sea is furrowed with the tracks of ships, and over all the roads and all the waters a continuous stream of people passes up and down—travelling, as they say, for their pleasure. What is it, I wonder, that they go out for to see? Some, it is very certain, are hunting the whole world over for the best hotels; they will mention with enthusiasm their recent journey through Russia, but when you come to question them, you will find that they have nothing to tell except that in Moscow they were really as comfortable as if they had been at home, and even more luxurious, for they had three varieties of game at the table of their host. Some have an eye fixed on the peculiarities of foreign modes of life, that they may gratify their patriotic hearts by condemning them when they differ (as they not infrequently do) from the English customs which they have left, and to which their thoughts turn regretfully; as I have heard the whole French nation summarily dismissed from the pale of civilization because they failed to perceive that boiled potatoes were an essential complement to the roast. To some travelling is merely the traversing of so many hundred miles; no matter whether not an inch of country, not an object of interest, remains in the eye of the mind—they have crossed a continent, they are travellers. These bring back with them only the names of the places they have visited, but are much concerned that the list should be a long one. They will cross over to Scutari that they may conscientiously say they have been in Asia, and traverse India from end to end that they may announce that they have visited all the tombs. They are full of expedients to lighten the hardships of a road whose varied pleasures have no charm for them. They will exhibit with pride their bulky luncheon-baskets, and cast withering glances at that humble flask of yours which has seen so many adventures over the edge of your coat-pocket. "Ah," they will say, "when you have travelled a little you will begin to learn how to make yourself comfortable." And you will hold your peace, and hug your flask and your adventures closer to your heart.

All these, and more also, are not travellers in the true sense of the word; they might as well have stayed at home and read a geography-book, or turned over a volume of photographs, and engaged a succession of cooks of different nationalities; but the real travellers, what pleasures are they seeking in fresh lands and strange cities? Reeds shaken in the wind are a picturesque foreground, but scarcely worth a day's journey into the wilderness; men clothed in soft raiment are not often to be met with in hotel or caravanserai, and as for prophets, there are as many at home, maybe, as in other places.

Well, every man carries a different pair of eyes with him, and no two people would answer the question in the same fashion. For myself, I am sometimes tempted to believe that the true pleasure of travel is to be derived from travelling companions. Such curious beings as you fall in with, and in such unexpected places! Although your acquaintance may be short in hours, it is long in experience; and when you part you feel as intimate as if you had shared the same slice of bread-and-butter in your nursery, and the same bottle of claret in your college hall. The vicissitudes of the road have a wonderful talent for bringing out the fine flavour of character. One day may show a man in as many different aspects as it would take ten years of customary life to exhibit. Moreover, time goes slowly on a ship or in a railway train, and a man is apt to better its pace by relating the incidents of his career to a sympathetic listener. In this manner the doors of palaces and of secret chambers in remote corners of the world fly open to you, and though you may have crossed no more unfamiliar waters than those of the North Sea, you pass through Petersburg and Bokhara, Poland and Algeria, on your way to Antwerp. English people are not so communicative, even abroad, and what they have to tell is of less interest if you are athirst for unknown conditions; their tales lack the charm of those which fall from the lips of men coming, as it were, out of a dream-world, crossing but once the glow of solid reality which lights your own path, and vanishing as suddenly as they came into space. Like packmen, we unfasten our wares, open our little bundle of experiences, spread them out and finger them over: the ship touches at the port, and silks and tinsel are gathered up and strapped upon our backs and carried—God knows where!

The man who carried the most amusing wares we ever examined was a Russian officer, and he spread them out for our inspection as we steamed round the eastern and northern coasts of the Black Sea. He was a magnificent creature, fair-haired, blue-eyed, broad-shouldered, and tall; he must have stood six feet four in those shining top boots of his. His beard was cut into a point, and his face was like that of some handsome, courteous seventeenth-century nobleman smiling out of a canvas of Vandyke's. He was a mighty hunter, so he told us; he lived with his wife and daughters out in Transcaspia, where he governed a province and hunted the lions and the wolves (and perhaps the Turkomans also) with packs of dogs and regiments of mounted huntsmen. He was writing a book about Transcaspia; there would be much, he said, of hunt in its pages. He spoke English, and hastened to inform us that every Russian of good family learnt English from his youth up. I trust that the number of his quarterings was in direct proportion to the number of grammatical errors he perpetrated in our tongue, for if so our friend must have been as well connected as he said he was. He told wonderful stories of the wealth and splendour of his family; all the great Slav houses and all their most ancient names seemed to be united in his person. His mother was Princess This, his wife was Princess That, his father had been a governor of such and such a province; he himself, until a few years back, was the most brilliant of the officers in the Czar's guards—indeed, he had only left Petersburg because, with a growing family, he could no longer afford to spend £40,000 a year (or some such sum—I remember it seemed to us enormous). "And you know," he added, "under £40,000 a year you cannot live in Petersburg—not as I am accustomed to live." So he had retired to economize among the lions and the Turkomans until his fortunes should retrieve themselves, which there was every prospect of their doing, since his wife was to inherit one of the largest properties in Russia and he himself would come into the second largest on the death of his mother. Of that lady he spoke with a gentle sorrow: "She is very miser," he would say whenever he alluded to her. "She send her blessing, but no pence!" We murmured words of sympathy, but he was not to be comforted—her avarice rankled. "Ah, yes," he sighed, when her name came up again in the course of conversation, "she is very miser!"

It may be that our agreeable companion did not consider himself to be bound by those strict rules of accuracy which tied in a measure our own tongues; his velvets may have been cotton-backed, and his diamonds paste, for all their glitter. We had the opportunity of testing only one of his statements, and I must confess that we were lamentably disappointed. One evening at dinner he was telling us of the prodigies of strength he had accomplished, how he had lifted men with one finger, thrown stupendous weights, and grappled with wild beasts of monstrous size. He even descended into further details. "In the house of my mother," he said, "I took a napkin and bent him twenty times and tore him across!" We were interested, and, to beguile the monotony of the evening, we begged him to perform the same feat on the captain's linen; he acceded, and after dinner we assembled on deck full of expectation. The napkin was produced and folded three or four times; he tore and tore—not a thread gave way! Again he pulled and wrenched until he was red in the face with pulling (and we with shame), and still the napkin was as united as ever. At length we offered some effete excuses—in the house of his mother, even though she was so very miser, the linen was probably of finer quality; no one could be expected to tear one of the ship's napkins, which was as coarse as sackcloth. He accepted the explanation, but nothing is so disconcerting as to be convicted of exaggeration,

and though we were heartily sorry for our indis-
cretion, our acquaintance never again touched
those planes of intimacy which it had reached
before. Next morning we arrived at Odessa, and
parted company with distant bows, nor will he
ever, I fear me, send us the promised volume
containing some description of Transcaspia and
much of hunt.

There is a curious reservation in the com-
municativeness of a Russian. He will tell you all
you wish to know (and more) of himself and of
his family, but once touch upon his country or
his Government and he is dumb. We noticed
this trait in another casual travelling acquaintance, who talked so freely of his own doings, and
even of more general topics, such as the novels
of Tolstoi, that we were encouraged to question
him concerning the condition of the peasantry.
"What of the famine?" we asked. "Famine!" he
said and a blank expression came over his face.
"I have heard of no famine—there is no famine
in Russia!" And yet credible witnesses had
informed us that people were dying by thousands
in the southern provinces, not so far removed
from Batoum, where our friend occupied a high
official position. Doubtless, if we had asked of
the Jews, he would have replied with the same

imperturbable face—"Jews! I have heard of no Jews in Russia!"

The charm of such friendships lies in their transient character. Before you have time to tire of the new acquaintances they are gone, and in all probability the discussion, which was beginning to grow a little tedious, will never be renewed. You meet them as you meet strangers at a dinner-table, but with less likelihood that the chances of fortune will throw you again together, and less within the trammels of social conventions. Ah, but for those conventions how often might one not sit beside the human being instead of beside the suit of evening clothes! People put on their indistinctive company manners with their indistinctive white shirt-fronts, and only once can I remember to have seen the man pierce through the dress. The transgressor was a Turkish secretary of legation. He was standing gloomily before a suppertable, eyeing the dishes with a hungry glance, when someone came up and asked him why he would not sup. "Ah," he sighed, "ma ceinture! Elle est tellement serrée que je ne puis rien manger!" There was a touch of human nature for you! The suffering Turk said nothing memorable for the rest of the evening, but his own remark brands itself upon the mind, and will not be easily forgotten. I have often wondered at what compromise he and his waistband have arrived during the elapsing years, which must, in spite of all his care, have added certain inches to his circumference.

Not with such fugitive acquaintanceships alone may your fellow-travellers beguile the way: there are many whom you never come to know, and who yet afford a delightful field for observation. In the East a man may travel with his whole family, and yet scarcely interrupt the common flow of every-day life, and by watching them you will learn much concerning Oriental habits which would never otherwise have penetrated through the harem walls. A Turk will arrive on board a ship with half a dozen of his women-kind and as many misshapen bundles, scarcely to be distinguished in form from the beveiled and becloaked ladies themselves. In the course of the next half-hour you will discover that these bundles contain the beds of the family, their food, and all the necessaries of life for the three or four days of the voyage. They will proceed presently to camp out on some portion of the deck roped off for their protection, spreading out their mat-tresses and their blankets under the open sky, performing what summary toilet they may under their feridgis, eating, sleeping, praying, conversing together, or playing with the pet birds they have brought with them, all in full view of the other passengers, but with as little heed to them as if the rope barrier were really the harem wall it simulates. Meantime, the grave lord of this troop of women paces the deck with dignified tread, and from time to time stops beside his wife and daughters and throws them a word of encouragement.

These family parties may prove of no small inconvenience to other passengers, as once when we were crossing the Sea of Marmora we found the whole of the upper deck cut off from us by an awning and canvas walls, and occupied by chattering women. We remonstrated, and were told that it was unavoidable; the women were great ladies, the family of the Governor of Brousa, with their attendants; they were going to Constantinople, there to celebrate the marriage of one of his daughters with the son of a wealthy pasha. Hence all the laughter and the subdued clatter of tongues, and the air of festive expectation which penetrated through cloaks and veils and canvas walls. But we, who had not the good fortune to be related to pashas, were obliged to content ourselves with the stairs which led on to the deck, on which we seated ourselves with the bad grace of Europeans who feel that they have been cheated of their rights.

Such comparative comfort is enjoyed only by the richer sort; for the poor a sea-voyage is a matter of considerable hardship. They, too, sleep on deck; down on the lower deck they spread their ragged matresses among ropes and casks and all the miscellaneous detritus of a ship, with the smell and the rattle of the engines in the midst of them, and their rest disturbed by the coming and going of sailors and the bustle of lading and unlading. They cook their own food, for they will not touch that which is prepared by Christian hands, and on chilly nights they seek what shelter they may under the warm funnels. We used to watch these fellow-travellers of ours upon the Caspian boat, setting forth their evening meal as the dusk closed in—it needed little preparation, but they devoured their onions and cheese and coarse sandy cakes of bread with no less relish, and scooped out the pink flesh of their water-melons until nothing but the thinnest paring of rind remained. And as we watched the strange dinner-party of rags and tatters, we fancied that we realized what the feelings of that hasty personage in the Bible must have been after he had gathered in the people from the highways and the byways to partake of his feast, and we congratulated ourselves that we were not called upon to sit as host among them.

Pilgrims from Mecca form a large proportion of the Oriental travellers on the Black Sea. There were two such men on our boat. They were Persians; they wore long Persian robes of dark hues, and on their heads the Persian hat of astrakhan; but you might have guessed their nationality by their faces—the pale, clear-cut Persian faces, with high, narrow foreheads, deep-set eyes and arching brows. They were always together, and held little or no converse with the other passengers, than whom they were clearly of a much higher social status. They stood in the ship's bow gazing eastward, as though they were already looking for the walls of their own Meshed on the far horizon, and perhaps they pondered over the accomplishment of the holy journey, and over the aspect of the sacred places which they, too, had seen at last, but I think their minds were occupied with the prospect of rejoining wife and children and Heimat out there in Meshed, and that was why their silent gaze was turned persistently eastward.

We tried to picture what miseries these people must undergo when storms sweep the crowded deck, and the wind blows through the tattered blankets, and the snow is bed-fellow on the hard mattresses; but for us the pleasant summer weather lies for ever on those inland seas, sun and clear starlight bathe coasts beautiful and desolate sloping down to green water, the playing-ground of porpoises, the evening meals are eaten under the clear skies we knew, and morning breaks fresh and cool through the soft mists to light mysterious lands and wonderful.

Finding Your
Path

HENRY DAVID THOREAU

Where I Lived, and What I Lived For

At a certain season of our life we are accustomed to consider every spot as the possible site of a house. I have thus surveyed the country on every side within a dozen miles of where I live. In imagination I have bought all the farms in succession, for all were to be bought, and I knew their price. I walked over each farmer's premises, tasted his wild apples, discoursed on husbandry with him, took his farm at his price, at any price, mortgaging it to him in my mind; even put a higher price on it,—took every thing but a deed of it,—took his word for his deed, for I dearly love to talk,—cultivated it, and him too to some extent, I trust, and withdrew when I had enjoyed it long enough, leaving him to carry it on. This experience entitled me to be regarded as a sort of real-estate broker by my friends. Wherever I sat, there I might live, and the landscape radiated from me accordingly. What is a house but a *sedes*, a seat?—better if a country seat. I discovered many a site for a house not likely to be soon improved, which some might have thought too far from the village, but to my eyes the village was too far from it. Well, there I might live, I said; and there I did live, for an hour, a summer and a winter life; saw how I could let the years run off, buffet the winter through, and see the spring come in. The future inhabitants of this region, wherever they may place their houses, may be sure that they have been anticipated. An afternoon sufficed to lay out the land into orchard, woodlot, and pasture, and to decide what fine oaks or pines should be left to stand before the door, and whence each blasted tree could be seen to the best advantage; and then I let it lie, fallow perchance, for a man is rich in proportion to the number of things which he can afford to let alone.

My imagination carried me so far that I even had the refusal of several farms,—the refusal was all I wanted,—but I never got my fingers burned by actual possession. The nearest that I came to actual possession was when I bought the Hollowell place, and had begun to sort my seeds, and collected materials with which to make a wheelbarrow to carry it on or off with; but before the owner gave me a deed of it, his wife—every man has such a wife—changed her mind and wished to keep it, and he offered me ten dollars to release him. Now, to speak the truth, I had but ten cents in the world, and it surpassed my arithmetic to tell, if I was that man who had ten cents, or who had a farm, or ten dollars, or all together. However, I let him keep the ten dollars and the farm too, for I had carried it far enough; or rather, to be generous, I sold him the farm for just what I gave for it, and, as he was not a rich man, made him a present of ten dollars, and still had my ten cents, and seeds, and materials for a wheelbarrow left. I found thus that I had been a rich man without any damage to my poverty. But I retained the landscape, and I have since annually carried off what it yielded without a wheelbarrow. With respect to landscapes,—

"I am monarch of all I *survey*,
My right there is none to dispute."

I have frequently seen a poet withdraw, having enjoyed the most valuable part of a farm, while the crusty farmer supposed that he had got a few wild apples only. Why, the owner does not know it for many years when a poet has put his farm in rhyme, the most admirable kind of invisible fence, has fairly impounded it, milked it, skimmed it, and got all the cream, and left the farmer only the skimmed milk.

The real attractions of the Hollowell farm, to me, were; its complete retirement, being about two miles from the village, half a mile from the nearest neighbor, and separated from the highway by a broad field; its bounding on the river, which the owner said protected it by its fogs from frosts in the spring, though that was nothing to me; the gray color and ruinous state of the house and barn, and the dilapidated fences, which put such an interval between me and the last occupant; the hollow and lichen-covered apple trees, gnawed by rabbits, showing what kind of neighbors I should have; but above all, the recollection I had of it from my earliest voyages up the river, when the house was concealed behind a dense grove of red maples, through which I heard the house-dog bark. I was in haste to buy it, before the proprietor finished getting out some rocks, cutting down the hollow apple trees, and grubbing up some young birches which had sprung up in the pasture, or, in short, had made any more of his improvements. To enjoy these advantages I was ready to carry it on; like Atlas, to take the world on my shoulders,—I never heard what compensation he received for that,—and do all those things which had no other motive or excuse but that I might pay for it and be unmolested in my possession of it; for I knew all the while that it would yield the most abundant crop of the kind I wanted if I could only afford to let it alone. But it turned out as I have said.

All that I could say, then, with respect to farming on a large scale, (I have always cultivated a garden,) was, that I had had my seeds ready. Many think that seeds improve with age. I have no doubt that time discriminates between the good and the bad; and when at last I shall plant, I shall be less likely to be disappointed. But I would say to my fellows, once for all, As long as possible live free and uncommitted. It makes but little difference whether you are committed to a farm or the county jail.

Old Cato, whose "De Re Rusticâ" is my "Cultivator," says, and the only translation I have seen makes sheer nonsense of the passage, "When you think of getting a farm, turn it thus in your mind, not to buy greedily; nor spare your pains to look at it, and do not think it enough to go round it once. The oftener you go there the more it will please you, if it is good." I think I shall not buy greedily, but go round and round it as long as I live, and be buried in it first, that it may please me the more at last.

The present was my next experiment of this kind, which I purpose to describe more at length; for convenience, putting the experience of two years into one. As I have said, I do not propose to write an ode to dejection, but to brag as lustily as chanticleer in the morning, standing on his roost, if only to wake my neighbors up.

When first I took up my abode in the woods, that is, began to spend my nights as well as days there, which, by accident, was on Independence day, or the fourth of July, 1845, my house was not finished for winter, but was merely a defence against the rain, without plastering or chimney, the walls being of rough weather-stained boards, with wide chinks, which made it cool at night. The upright white hewn studs and freshly planed door and window casings gave it a clean and airy look, especially in the morning, when its timbers were saturated with dew, so that I fancied that by noon some sweet gum would exude from them. To my imagination it retained throughout the day more or less of this auroral character, reminding me of a certain house on a mountain which I had visited the year before. This was an airy and unplastered cabin, fit to entertain a travelling god, and where a goddess might trail her garments. The winds which passed over my dwelling were such as sweep over the ridges of mountains, bearing the broken strains, or celestial parts only, of terrestrial music. The morning wind forever blows, the poem of creation is uninterrupted; but few are the ears that hear it. Olympus is but the outside of the earth every where.

The only house I had been the owner of before, if I except a boat, was a tent, which I used occasionally when making excursions in the summer, and this is still rolled up in my garret; but the boat, after passing from hand to hand, has gone down the stream of time. With this more substantial shelter about me, I had made some progress toward settling in the world. This frame, so slightly clad, was a sort of crystallization around me, and reacted on the builder. It was suggestive somewhat as a picture in outlines. I did not need to go out doors to take the air, for the atmosphere within had lost none of its freshness. It was not so much within doors as behind a door where I sat, even in the rainiest weather. The Harivansa says, "An abode without birds is like a meat without seasoning." Such was not my abode, for I found myself suddenly neighbor to the birds; not by having imprisoned one, but having caged myself near them. I was not only nearer to some of those which commonly frequent the garden and the orchard, but to those wilder and more thrilling songsters of the forest which never, or rarely, serenade a villager,—the wood-thrush, the veery, the scarlet tanager, the field-sparrow, the whippoorwill, and many others.

I was seated by the shore of a small pond, about a mile and a half south of the village of Concord and somewhat higher than it, in the midst of an extensive wood between that town and Lincoln, and about two miles south of that our only field known to fame, Concord Battle Ground; but I was so low in the woods that the opposite shore, half a mile off, like the rest, covered with wood, was my most distant horizon. For the first week, whenever I looked out on the pond it impressed me like a tarn high up on the side of a mountain, its bottom far above the surface of other lakes, and, as the sun arose, I saw it throwing off its nightly clothing of mist, and here and there, by degrees, its soft ripples or its smooth reflecting surface was revealed, while the mists, like ghosts, were stealthily withdrawing in every direction into the woods, as at the breaking up of some nocturnal conventicle. The very dew seemed to hang upon the trees later into the day than usual, as on the sides of mountains.

This small lake was of most value as a neighbor in the intervals of a gentle rain storm in August, when, both air and water being perfectly still, but the sky overcast, mid-afternoon had all the serenity of evening, and the wood-thrush sang around, and was heard from shore to shore. A lake like this is never smoother than at such a time; and the clear portion of the air above it being shallow and darkened by clouds, the water, full of light and reflections, becomes a lower heaven itself so much the more important. From a hill top near by, where the wood had been recently cut off, there was a pleasing vista southward across the pond, through a wide indentation in the hills which form the shore there, where their opposite sides sloping toward each other suggested a stream flowing out in that direction through a wooded valley, but stream there was none. That way I looked between and over the near green hills to some distant and higher ones in the horizon, tinged with blue. Indeed, by standing on tiptoe I could catch a glimpse of some of the peaks of the still bluer and more distant mountain ranges in the north-west, those true-blue coins from heaven's own mint, and also of some portion of the village. But in other directions, even from this point, I could not see over or beyond the woods which surrounded me. It is well to have some water in your neighborhood, to give buoyancy to and float the earth. One value even of the smallest well is, that when you look into it you see that earth is not continent but insular. This is as important as that it keeps butter cool. When I looked across the pond from this peak toward the Sudbury meadows, which in time of flood I distinguished elevated perhaps by a mirage in their seething valley, like a coin in a basin, all the earth beyond the pond appeared like a thin crust insulated and floated even by this small sheet of intervening water, and I was reminded that this on which I dwelt was but *dry land*.

Though the view from my door was still more contracted, I did not feel crowded or confined in the least. There was pasture enough for my imagination. The low shrub-oak plateau to which the opposite shore arose, stretched away toward the prairies of the West and the steppes of Tartary, affording ample room for all the roving families of men. "There are none happy in the world but beings who enjoy freely a vast horizon,"—said

Damodara, when his herds required new and larger pastures.

Both place and time were changed, and I dwelt nearer to those parts of the universe and to those eras in history which had most attracted me. Where I lived was as far off as many a region viewed nightly by astronomers. We are wont to imagine rare and delectable places in some remote and more celestial corner of the system, behind the constellation of Cassiopeia's Chair, far from noise and disturbance. I discovered that my house actually had its site in such a withdrawn, but forever new and unprofaned, part of the universe. If it were worth the while to settle in those parts near to the Pleiades or the Hyades, to Aldebaran or Altair, then I was really there, or at an equal remoteness from the life which I had left behind, dwindled and twinkling with as fine a ray to my nearest neighbor, and to be seen only in moonless nights by him. Such was that part of creation where I had squatted;—

"There was a shepherd that did live,
    And held his thoughts as high
As were the mounts whereon his flocks
    Did hourly feed him by."

What should we think of the shepherd's life if his flocks always wandered to higher pastures than his thoughts?

Every morning was a cheerful invitation to make my life of equal simplicity, and I may say innocence, with Nature herself. I have been as sincere a worshipper of Aurora as the Greeks. I got up early and bathed in the pond; that was a religious exercise, and one of the best things which I did. They say that characters were engraven on the bathing tub of king Tehing-thang to this effect: "Renew thyself completely each day; do it again, and again, and forever again." I can understand that. Morning brings back the heroic ages. I was as much affected by the faint hum of a mosquito making its invisible and unimaginable tour through my apartment at earliest dawn, when I was sitting with door and windows open, as I could be by any trumpet that ever sang of fame. It was Homer's requiem; itself an Iliad and Odyssey in the air, singing its own wrath and wanderings. There was something cosmical about it; a standing advertisement, till forbidden, of the everlasting vigor and fertility of the world. The morning, which is the most memorable season of the day, is the awakening hour. Then there is least somnolence in us; and for an hour, at least, some part of us awakes which slumbers all the rest of the day and night. Little is to be expected of that day, if it can be called a day, to which we are not awakened by our Genius, but by the mechanical nudgings of some servitor, are not awakened by our own newly-acquired force and aspirations from within, accompanied by the undulations of celestial music, instead of factory bells, and a fragrance filling the air—to a higher life than we fell asleep from; and thus the darkness bear its fruit, and prove itself to be good, no less than the light. That man who does not believe that each day contains an earlier, more sacred, and auroral hour than he has yet profaned, has despaired of life, and is pursuing a descending and darkening way. After a partial cessation of his sensuous life, the soul of man, or its organs rather, are reinvigorated each day, and his Genius tries again what noble life it can make. All memorable events, I should say, transpire in morning time and in a morning atmosphere. The Vedas say, "All intelligences awake with the morning." Poetry and art, and the fairest and most memorable of the actions of men, date from such an hour. All poets and heroes, like Memnon, are the children of Aurora, and emit their music at sunrise. To him whose elastic and vigorous thought keeps pace with the sun, the day is a perpetual morning. It matters not what the clocks say or the attitudes and labors of men. Morning is when I am awake and there is a dawn in me. Moral reform is the effort to throw off sleep. Why is it that men give so poor an account of their day if they have not been slumbering? They are not such poor calculators. If they had not been overcome with drowsiness they would have performed something. The millions are awake enough for physical labor; but only one in a million is awake enough for effective intellectual exertion, only one in a hundred millions to a poetic or divine life. To be awake is to be alive. I have never yet met a man who was quite awake. How could I have looked him in the face?

We must learn to reawaken and keep ourselves awake, not by mechanical aids, but by an infinite expectation of the dawn, which does not forsake us in our soundest sleep. I know of no more encouraging fact than the unquestionable ability of man to elevate his life by a conscious endeavor. It is something to be able to paint a particular picture, or to carve a statue, and so to make a few objects beautiful; but it is far more glorious to carve and paint the very atmosphere and medium through which we look, which morally we can do. To affect the quality of the day, that is the highest of arts. Every man is tasked to make his life, even in its details, worthy of the contemplation of his most elevated and critical hour. If we refused, or rather used up, such paltry information as we get, the oracles would distinctly inform us how this might be done.

I went to the woods because I wished to live deliberately, to front only the essential facts of life, and see if I could not learn what it had to teach, and not, when I came to die, discover that I had not lived. I did not wish to live what was not life, living is so dear; nor did I wish to practise resignation, unless it was quite necessary. I wanted to live deep and suck out all the marrow of life, to live so sturdily and Spartan-like as to put to rout all that was not life, to cut a broad swath and shave close, to drive life into a corner, and reduce it to its lowest terms, and, if it proved to be mean, why then to get the whole and genuine meanness of it, and publish its meanness to the world; or if it were sublime, to know it by experience, and be able to give a true account of it in my next excursion. For most men, it appears to me, are in a strange uncertainty about it, whether it is of the devil or of God, and have *some-what hastily* concluded that it is the chief end of man here to "glorify God and enjoy him forever."

Still we live meanly, like ants; though the fable tells us that we were long ago changed into men; like pygmies we fight with cranes; it is error upon error, and clout upon clout, and our best virtue has for its occasion a superfluous and evitable wretchedness. Our life is frittered away by detail. An honest man has hardly need to count more than his ten fingers, or in extreme cases he may add his ten toes, and lump the rest. Simplicity, simplicity, simplicity! I say, let your affairs be as two or three, and not a hundred or a thousand; instead of a million count half a dozen, and keep your accounts on your thumb nail. In the midst of this chopping sea of civilized life, such are the clouds and storms and quick-sands and thousand-and-one items to be allowed for, that a man has to live, if he would not founder and go to the bottom and not make his port at all, by dead reckoning, and he must be a great calculator indeed who succeeds. Simplify, simplify. Instead of three meals a day, if it be necessary eat but one; instead of a hundred dishes, five; and reduce other things in proportion. Our life is like a German Confederacy, made up of petty states, with its boundary forever fluctuating, so that even a German cannot tell you how it is bounded at any moment. The nation itself, with all its so called internal improvements, which, by the way, are all external and superficial, is just such an unwieldy and overgrown establishment, cluttered with furniture and tripped up by its own traps, ruined by luxury and heedless expense, by want of calculation and a worthy aim, as the million households in the land; and the only cure for it as for them is in a rigid economy, a stern and more than Spartan simplicity of life and elevation of purpose. It lives too fast. Men think that it is essential that the *Nation* have commerce, and export ice, and talk through a telegraph, and ride thirty miles an hour, without a doubt, whether *they* do or not; but whether we should live like baboons or like men, is a little uncertain. If we do not get out sleepers, and forge rails, and devote days and nights to the work, but go to tinkering upon our *lives* to improve *them*, who will build railroads? And if railroads are not built, how shall we get to heaven in season? But if we stay at home and mind our business, who will want railroads? We do not ride on the railroad; it rides upon us. Did you ever think what those sleepers are that underlie the railroad? Each one is a man, an Irishman, or a Yankee man. The rails are laid on them, and they are covered with sand, and the cars run smoothly over them. They are sound sleepers, I assure you. And every few years a new lot is laid down and run over; so that, if some have the pleasure of riding on a rail, others have the misfortune to be ridden upon. And when they run over a man that is walking in his sleep, a supernumerary sleeper in the wrong position, and wake him up, they suddenly stop the cars, and make a hue and cry about it, as if this were an exception. I am glad to know that it takes a gang of men for every five miles to keep the sleepers down and level in their beds as it is, for this is a sign that they may sometime get up again.

Why should we live with such hurry and waste of life? We are determined to be starved before we are hungry. Men say that a stitch in time saves nine, and so they take a thousand stitches to-day to save nine tomorrow. As for *work*, we haven't any of any consequence. We have the Saint Vitus' dance, and cannot possibly keep our heads still. If I should only give a few pulls at the parish bell-rope, as for a fire, that is, without setting the bell, there is hardly a man on his farm in the outskirts of Concord, notwithstanding that press of engagements which was his excuse so many times this morning, nor a boy, nor a woman, I might almost say, but would forsake all and follow that sound, not mainly to save property from the flames, but, if we will confess the truth, much more to see it burn, since burn it must, and we, be it known, did not set it on fire,—or to see it put out, and have a hand in it, if that is done as handsomely; yes, even if it were the parish church itself. Hardly a man takes a half hour's nap after dinner, but when he wakes he holds up his head and asks, "What's the news?" as if the rest of mankind had stood his sentinels. Some give directions to be waked every half hour, doubtless for no other purpose; and then, to pay for it, they tell what they have dreamed. After a night's sleep the news is as indispensable as the breakfast. "Pray tell me any thing new that has happened to a man any where on this globe,"— and he reads it over his coffee and rolls, that a man has had his eyes gouged out this morning on the Wachito River; never dreaming the while that he lives in the dark unfathomed mammoth cave of this world, and has but the rudiment of an eye himself.

For my part, I could easily do without the post-office. I think that there are very few important communications made through it. To speak critically, I never received more than one or two letters in my life—I wrote this some years ago— that were worth the postage. The penny-post is, commonly, an institution through which you seriously offer a man that penny for his thoughts which is so often safely offered in jest. And I am sure that I never read any memorable news in a newspaper. If we read of one man robbed, or murdered, or killed by accident, or one house burned, or one vessel wrecked, or one steamboat blown up, or one cow run over on the Western Railroad, or one mad dog killed, or one lot of grasshoppers in the winter,—we never need read of another. One is enough. If you are acquainted with the principle, what do you care for a myriad instances and applications? To a philosopher all *news*, as it is called, is gossip, and they who edit and read it are old women over their tea. Yet not a few are greedy after this gossip. There was such a rush, as I hear, the other day at one of the offices to learn the foreign news by the last arrival, that several large squares of plate glass belonging to the establishment were broken by the pressure,—news which I seriously think a ready wit might write a twelvemonth or twelve years beforehand with sufficient accuracy. As for Spain, for instance, if you know how to throw in Don Carlos and the Infanta, and Don Pedro and Seville and Granada, from time to time in the right proportions,—they may have changed the names a little since I saw the papers,—and serve up a bull-fight when other entertainments fail, it will be true to the letter, and give us as good an idea of the exact state or ruin of things in Spain as the most succinct and lucid reports under this head in the newspapers: and as for England, almost the last significant scrap of news from that quarter was the revolution of 1649; and if you have learned the history of her crops for an average year, you never need attend to that thing again, unless your speculations are of a merely pecuniary character. If one may judge who rarely looks into the newspapers, nothing new does ever happen in foreign parts, a French revolution not excepted.

What news! how much more important to know what that is which was never old! "Kieouhe-yu (great dignitary of the state of Wei) sent a man to Kloung-tseu to know his news. Khoungtscu caused the messenger to be seated near him, and questioned him in these terms: What is your master doing? The messenger answered with respect: My master desires to diminish the number of his faults, but he cannot come to the end of them. The messenger being gone, the philosopher remarked: What a worthy messenger! What a worthy messenger!" The preacher, instead of vexing the ears of drowsy farmers on their day of rest at the end of the week,—for Sunday is the fit conclusion of an ill-spent week, and not the fresh and brave beginning of a new one,—with this one other draggletail of a sermon, should shout with thundering voice,—"Pause! Avast! Why so seeming fast, but deadly slow?"

Shams and delusions are esteemed for soundest truths, while reality is fabulous. If men would steadily observe realities only, and not allow themselves to be deluded, life, to compare it with such things as we know, would be like a fairy tale and the Arabian Nights' Entertainments. If we respected only what is inevitable and has a right to be, music and poetry would resound along the streets. When we are unhurried and wise, we perceive that only great and worthy things have any permanent and absolute existence,—that petty fears and petty pleasures are but the shadow of the reality. This is always exhilarating and sublime. By closing the eyes and slumbering, and consenting to be deceived by shows, men establish and confirm their daily life of routine and habit every where, which still is built on purely illusory foundations. Children, who play life, discern its true law and relations more clearly than men, who fail to live it worthily, but who think that they are wiser by experience, that is, by failure. I have read in a Hindoo book, that "there was a king's son, who, being expelled in infancy from his native city, was brought up by a forester, and, growing up to maturity in that state, imagined himself to belong to the barbarous race with which he lived. One of his father's ministers having discovered him, revealed to him what he was, and the misconception of his character was removed, and he knew himself to be a prince. So soul," continues the Hindoo philosopher, "from the circumstances in which it is placed, mistakes its own character, until the truth is revealed to it by some holy teacher, and then it knows itself to be *Brahme*." I perceive that we inhabitants of New England live this mean life that we do because our vision does not penetrate the surface of things. We think that that *is* which *appears* to be. If a man should walk through this town and see only the reality, where, think you, would the "Mill-dam" go to? If he should give us an account of the realities he beheld there, we should not recognize the place in his description. Look at a meeting-house, or a court-house, or a jail, or a shop, or a dwelling-house, and say what that thing really is before a true gaze, and they would all go to pieces in your account of them. Men esteem truth remote, in the outskirts of the system, behind the farthest star, before Adam and after the last man. In eternity there is indeed something true and sublime. But all these times and places and occasions are now and here. God himself culminates in the present moment, and will never be more divine in the lapse of all the ages. And we are enabled to apprehend at all what is sublime and noble only by the perpetual instilling and drenching of the reality that surrounds us. The universe constantly and obediently answers to our conceptions; whether we travel fast or slow, the track is laid for us. Let us spend our lives in conceiving then. The poet or the artist never yet had so fair and noble a design but some of his posterity at least could accomplish it.

Let us spend one day as deliberately as Nature, and not be thrown off the track by every nutshell and mosquito's wing that falls on the rails. Let us rise early and fast, or break fast, gently and without perturbation; let company come and let company go, let the bells ring and the children cry,—determined to make a day of it. Why should we knock under and go with the stream? Let us not be upset and overwhelmed in that terrible rapid and whirlpool called a dinner, situated in the meridian shallows. Weather this danger and you are safe, for the rest of the way is down hill.

With unrelaxed nerves, with morning vigor, sail by it, looking another way, tied to the mast like Ulysses. If the engine whistles, let it whistle till it is hoarse for its pains. If the bell rings, why should we run? We will consider what kind of music they are like. Let us settle ourselves, and work and wedge our feet downward through the mud and slush of opinion, and prejudice, and tradition, and delusion, and appearance, that alluvion which covers the globe, through Paris and London, through New York and Boston and Concord, through church and state, through poetry and philosophy and religion, till we come to a hard bottom and rocks in place, which we can call *reality*, and say, This is, and no mistake; and then begin, having a *point d'appui*, below freshet and frost and fire, a place where you might found a wall or a state, or set a lamp-post safely, or perhaps a gauge, not a Nilometer, but a Realometer, that future ages might know how deep a freshet of shams and appearances had gathered from time to time. If you stand right fronting and face to face to a fact, you will see the sun glimmer on both its surfaces, as if it were a cimeter, and feel its sweet edge dividing you through the heart and marrow, and so you will happily conclude your mortal career. Be it life or death, we crave only reality. If we are really dying, let us hear the rattle in our throats and feel cold in the extremities; if we are alive, let us go about our business.

Time is but the stream I go a-fishing in. I drink at it; but while I drink I see the sandy bottom and detect how shallow it is. Its thin current slides away, but eternity remains. I would drink deeper; fish in the sky, whose bottom is pebbly with stars. I cannot count one. I know not the first letter of the alphabet. I have always been regretting that I was not as wise as the day I was born. The intellect is a cleaver; it discerns and rifts its way into the secret of things. I do not wish to be any more busy with my hands than is necessary. My head is hands and feet. I feel all my best faculties concentrated in it. My instinct tells me that my head is an organ for burrowing, as some creatures use their snout and fore-paws, and with it I would mine and burrow my way through these hills. I think that the richest vein is somewhere hereabouts; so by the divining rod and thin rising vapors I judge; and here I will begin to mine.

MARK TWAIN

Advice to Youth

ABOUT 1882

Being told I would be expected to talk here, I inquired what sort of a talk I ought to make. They said it should be something suitable to youth—something didactic, instructive, or something in the nature of good advice. Very well. I have a few things in my mind which I have often longed to say for the instruction of the young; for it is in one's tender early years that such things will best take root and be most enduring and most valuable. First, then, I will say to you, my young friends—and I say it beseechingly, urgingly—

Always obey your parents, when they are present. This is the best policy in the long run, because if you don't they will make you. Most parents think they know better than you do, and you can generally make more by humoring that superstition than you can by acting on your own better judgment.

Be respectful to your superiors, if you have any, also to strangers, and sometimes to others. If a person offend you, and you are in doubt as to whether it was intentional or not, do not resort to extreme measures; simply watch your chance and hit him with a brick. That will be sufficient. If you shall find that he had not intended any offense, come out frankly and confess yourself in the wrong when you struck him; acknowledge it like a man and say you didn't mean to. Yes, always avoid violence; in this age of charity and kindliness, the time has gone by for such things. Leave dynamite to the low and unrefined.

Go to bed early, get up early—this is wise. Some authorities say get up with the sun; some others say get up with one thing, some with another. But a lark is really the best thing to get up with. It gives you a splendid reputation with everybody to know that you get up with the lark; and if you get the right kind of a lark, and work at him right, you can easily train him to get up at half past nine, every time—it is no trick at all.

Now as to the matter of lying. You want to be very careful about lying; otherwise you are nearly sure to get caught. Once caught, you can never again be, in the eyes of the good and the pure, what you were before. Many a young person has injured himself permanently through a single clumsy and ill-finished lie, the result of carelessness born of incomplete training. Some authorities hold that the young ought not to lie at all. That, of course, is putting it rather stronger than necessary; still, while I cannot go quite so far as that, I do maintain, and I believe I am right, that the young ought to be temperate in the use of this great art until practice and experience shall give them that confidence, elegance, and precision which alone can make the accomplishment graceful and profitable. Patience, diligence, painstaking attention to detail—these are the requirements; these, in time, will make the student perfect; upon these, and upon these only, may he rely as the sure foundation for future eminence. Think what tedious years of study, thought, practice, experience, went to the equipment of that peerless old master who was able to impose upon the whole world the lofty and sounding maxim that "truth is mighty and will prevail"—the most majestic compound fracture of fact which any of woman born has yet achieved. For the history of our race, and each individual's experience, are sown thick with evidence that a truth is not hard to kill and that a lie told well is immortal. There in Boston is a monument of the man who discovered anæsthesia; many people are aware, in these latter days, that that man didn't discover it at all, but stole the discovery from another man. Is this truth mighty, and will it prevail? Ah no, my hearers, the monument is made of hardy material, but the lie it tells will outlast it a million years. An awkward, feeble, leaky lie is a thing which you ought to make it your unceasing study to avoid; such a lie as that has no more real permanence than an average truth. Why, you might as well tell the truth at once and be done with it. A feeble, stupid, preposterous lie will not live two years—except it be a slander upon somebody. It is indestructible, then, of course, but that is no merit of yours. A final word: begin your practice of this gracious and beautiful art early—begin now. If I had begun earlier, I could have learned how.

Never handle firearms carelessly. The sorrow and suffering that have been caused through the innocent but heedless handling of firearms by the young! Only four days ago, right in the next farmhouse to the one where I am spending the summer, a grandmother, old and gray and sweet, one of the loveliest spirits in the land, was sitting at her work, when her young grandson crept in and got down an old, battered, rusty gun which had not been touched for many years and was supposed not to be loaded, and pointed it at her, laughing and threatening to shoot. In her fright she ran screaming and pleading toward the door on the other side of the room; but as she passed him he placed the gun almost against her very breast and pulled the trigger! He had supposed it was not loaded. And he was right—it wasn't. So there wasn't any harm done. It is the only case of that kind I ever heard of. Therefore, just the same, don't you meddle with old unloaded firearms; they are the most deadly and unerring things that have ever been created by man. You don't have to take any pains at all with them; you don't have to have a rest, you don't have to have any sights on the gun, you don't have to take aim, even. No, you just pick out a relative and bang away, and you are sure to get him. A youth who can't hit a cathedral at thirty yards with a Gatling gun in three-quarters of an hour, can take up an old empty musket and bag his grandmother every time, at a hundred. Think what Waterloo would have been if one of the armies had been boys armed with old muskets supposed not to be loaded, and the other army had been composed of their female relations. The very thought of it makes one shudder.

There are many sorts of books; but good ones are the sort for the young to read. Remember that. They are a great, an inestimable, an unspeakable means of improvement. Therefore be careful in your selection, my young friends; be very careful; confine yourselves exclusively to Robertson's Sermons, Baxter's *Saint's Rest*, *The Innocents Abroad*, and works of that kind.

But I have said enough. I hope you will treasure up the instructions which I have given you, and make them a guide to your feet and a light to your understanding. Build your character thoughtfully and painstaking upon these precepts, and by and by, when you have got it built, you will be surprised and gratified to see how nicely and sharply it resembles everybody else's.

WALT WHITMAN

Song of the Open Road

1

A foot and light-hearted I take to the
    open road,
Healthy, free, the world before me,
The long brown path before me leading
    wherever I choose.
Henceforth I ask not good-fortune, I myself
    am good-fortune,
Henceforth I whimper no more, postpone no
    more, need nothing,
Done with indoor complaints, libraries,
    querulous criticisms,
Strong and content I travel the open road.

The earth, that is sufficient,
I do not want the constellations any nearer,
I know they are very well where they are,

I know they suffice for those who belong
   to them.

(Still here I carry my old delicious burdens,
I carry them, men and women, I carry them
   with me wherever I go,
I swear it is impossible for me to get rid
   of them,
I am fill'd with them, and I will fill them
   in return.)

2

You road I enter upon and look around,
   I believe you are not all that is here,
I believe that much unseen is also here.

Here the profound lesson of reception, nor
   preference nor denial,
The black with his woolly head, the felon,
   the diseas'd, the illiterate person, are not
   denied;
The birth, the hasting after the physician, the
   beggar's tramp, the drunkard's
   stagger, the laughing party of mechanics,
The escaped youth, the rich person's
   carriage, the fop, the eloping couple,

The early market-man, the hearse, the moving
    of furniture into the town, the return back
    from the town,
They pass, I also pass, any thing passes, none
    can be interdicted,
None but are accepted, none but shall be dear
    to me.

3

You air that serves me with breath to speak!
You objects that call from diffusion my
    meanings and give them shape!
You light that wraps me and all things in
    delicate equable showers!
You paths worn in the irregular hollows by the
    roadsides!
I believe you are latent with unseen existences,
    you are so dear to me.

You flagg'd walks of the cities! you strong
    curbs at the edges!
You ferries! you planks and posts of wharves!
    you timber-lined sides! you distant ships!
You rows of houses! you window-pierc'd
    façades! you roofs!

You porches and entrances! you copings and
    iron guards!
You windows whose transparent shells might
    expose so much!
You doors and ascending steps! you arches!
You gray stones of interminable pavements!
    you trodden crossings!
From all that has touch'd you I believe you
    have imparted to yourselves, and now
    would impart the same secretly to me,
From the living and the dead you have
    peopled your impassive surfaces, and the
    spirits thereof would be evident and
    amicable with me.

4

The earth expanding right hand and left hand,
The picture alive, every part in its best light,
The music falling in where it is wanted, and
    stopping where it is not wanted,
The cheerful voice of the public road, the gay
    fresh sentiment of the road.

O highway I travel, do you say to me *Do not
leave me?*

Do you say *Venture not—if you leave me you are lost?*

Do you say *I am already prepared, I am well-beaten and undenied, adhere to me?*

O public road, I say back I am not afraid to leave you, yet I love you,

You express me better than I can express myself,

You shall be more to me than my poem.

I think heroic deeds were all conceiv'd in the open air, and all free poems also,

I think I could stop here myself and do miracles,

I think whatever I shall meet on the road I shall like, and whoever beholds me shall like me,

I think whoever I see must be happy.

5

From this hour I ordain myself loos'd of limits and imaginary lines,

Going where I list, my own master total and absolute,

Listening to others, considering well what they say,

Pausing, searching, receiving, contemplating,

Gently, but with undeniable will, divesting
    myself of the holds that would hold me.
I inhale great draughts of space,
The east and the west are mine, and the north
    and the south are mine.

I am larger, better than I thought,
I did not know I held so much goodness.

All seems beautiful to me,
I can repeat over to men and women You have
    done such good to me I would do the same
    to you,
I will recruit for myself and you as I go,
I will scatter myself among men and women
    as I go,
I will toss a new gladness and roughness
    among them,
Whoever denies me it shall not trouble me,
Whoever accepts me he or she shall be blessed
    and shall bless me.

6

Now if a thousand perfect men were to appear
    it would not amaze me,

Now if a thousand beautiful forms of women
    appear'd it would not astonish me.
Now I see the secret of the making of the best
    persons,
It is to grow in the open air and to eat and
    sleep with the earth.

Here a great personal deed has room,
(Such a deed seizes upon the hearts of the
    whole race of men,
Its effusion of strength and will overwhelms
    law and mocks all authority and all
    argument against it.)

Here is the test of wisdom,
Wisdom is not finally tested in schools,
Wisdom cannot be pass'd from one having it
    to another not having it,
Wisdom is of the soul, is not susceptible of
    proof, is its own proof,
Applies to all stages and objects and
    qualities and is content,
Is the certainty of the reality and
    immortality of things, and the excellence of
    things;
Something there is in the float of the sight of
    things that provokes it out of the soul.

Now I re-examine philosophies and religions,
They may prove well in lecture-rooms, yet not
    prove at all under the spacious clouds and
    along the landscape and flowing currents.
Here is realization,
Here is a man tallied—he realizes here what
    he has in him,
The past, the future, majesty, love—if they are
    vacant of you, you are vacant of them.

Only the kernel of every object nourishes;
Where is he who tears off the husks for you
    and me?
Where is he that undoes stratagems and
    envelopes for you and me?

Here is adhesiveness, it is not previously
    fashion'd, it is apropos;
Do you know what it is as you pass to be
    loved by strangers?
Do you know the talk of those turning
    eye-balls?

7

Here is the efflux of the soul,

The efflux of the soul comes from within
through embower'd gates, ever provoking
questions,
These yearnings why are they? these thoughts
in the darkness why are they?
Why are there men and women that while
they are nigh me the sunlight expands my
blood?
Why when they leave me do my pennants of
joy sink flat and lank?
Why are there trees I never walk under but
large and melodious thoughts descend
upon me?
(I think they hang there winter and summer
on those trees and always drop fruit as I
pass;)
What is it I interchange so suddenly with
strangers?
What with some driver as I ride on the seat
by his side?
What with some fisherman drawing his seine
by the shore as I walk by and pause?
What gives me to be free to a woman's and
man's good-will? what gives them to be
free to mine?

8

The efflux of the soul is happiness, here is
    happiness,
I think it pervades the open air, waiting at all
    times,
Now it flows unto us, we are rightly charged.

Here rises the fluid and attaching character,
The fluid and attaching character is the
    freshness and sweetness of man and
    woman,
(The herbs of the morning sprout no fresher
    and sweeter every day out of the roots of
    themselves, than it sprouts fresh and sweet
    continually out of itself.)

Toward the fluid and attaching character
    exudes the sweat of the love of young
    and old,
From it falls distill'd the charm that mocks
    beauty and attainments, Toward it
    heaves the shuddering longing ache of
    contact.

9

Allons! whoever you are come travel with me!
Traveling with me you find what never tires.

The earth never tires,
The earth is rude, silent, incomprehensible at
    first, Nature is rude and incomprehensible
    at first,
Be not discouraged, keep on, there are divine
    things well envelop'd,
I swear to you there are divine things more
    beautiful than words can tell.

Allons! we must not stop here,
However sweet these laid-up stores, however
    convenient this dwelling we cannot remain
    here,
However shelter'd this port and however calm
    these waters we must not anchor here,
However welcome the hospitality that
    surrounds us we are permitted to receive it
    but a little while.

10

Allons! the inducements shall be greater,

171

We will sail pathless and wild seas,
We will go where winds blow, waves dash,
and the Yankee clipper speeds by under
full sail.

Allons! with power, liberty, the earth, the
elements,
Health, defiance, gayety, self-esteem,
curiosity;
Allons! from all formules!
From your formules, O bat-eyed and
materialistic priests.

The stale cadaver blocks up the passage—the
burial waits no longer.
Allons! yet take warning!
He traveling with me needs the best blood,
thews, endurance,
None may come to the trial till he or she
bring courage and health,
Come not here if you have already spent the
best of yourself,
Only those may come who come in sweet and
determin'd bodies,
No diseas'd person, no rum-drinker or
venereal taint is permitted here.

(I and mine do not convince by arguments,
    similes, rhymes,
We convince by our presence.)

11

Listen! I will be honest with you,
I do not offer the old smooth prizes, but offer
    rough new prizes,
These are the days that must happen to you:
You shall not heap up what is call'd riches,
You shall scatter with lavish hand all that you
    earn or achieve,
You but arrive at the city to which you were
    destin'd, you hardly settle yourself to
    satisfaction before you are call'd by an
    irresistible call to depart,
You shall be treated to the ironical smiles and
    mockings of those who remain behind you,
What beckonings of love you receive you
    shall only answer with passionate kisses of
    parting,
You shall not allow the hold of those who
    spread their reach'd hands toward you.

12

Allons! after the great Companions, and to
    belong to them!
They too are on the road—they are the swift
    and majestic men—they are the greatest
    women,
Enjoyers of calms of seas and storms of seas,
Sailors of many a ship, walkers of many a mile
    of land,
Habituès of many distant countries, habituès
    of far-distant dwellings,
Trusters of men and women, observers
    of cities, solitary toilers,
Pausers and contemplators of tufts,
    blossoms, shells of the shore,
Dancers at wedding-dances, kissers of brides,
    tender helpers of children, bearers of
    children,
Soldiers of revolts, standers by gaping graves,
    lowerers-down of coffins,
Journeyers over consecutive seasons, over the
    years, the curious years each emerging
    from that which preceded it,
Journeyers as with companions, namely their
    own diverse phases,

Forth-steppers from the latent unrealized
  baby-days,
Journeyers gayly with their own youth,
  journeyers with their bearded and
  well-grain'd manhood,
Journeyers with their womanhood, ample,
  unsurpass'd, content,
Journeyers with their own sublime old age of
  manhood or womanhood,
Old age, calm, expanded, broad with the
  haughty breadth of the universe,
Old age, flowing free with the delicious
  near-by freedom of death.

13

Allons! to that which is endless as it was
  beginningless,
To undergo much, tramps of days, rests of
  nights,
To merge all in the travel they tend to, and
  the days and nights they tend to,
Again to merge them in the start of superior
  journeys,
To see nothing anywhere but what you may
  reach it and pass it,

To conceive no time, however distant,
　　but what you may reach it and pass it,
To look up or down no road but it stretches
　　and waits for you, however long but it
　　stretches and waits for you,
To see no being, not God's or any, but you
　　also go thither,
To see no possession but you may possess
　　it, enjoying all without labor or purchase,
　　abstracting the feast yet not abstracting one
　　particle of it,
To take the best of the farmer's farm and the
　　rich man's elegant villa, and the chaste
　　blessings of the well-married couple,
　　and the fruits of orchards and flowers of
　　gardens,
To take to your use out of the compact cities
　　as you pass through,
To carry buildings and streets with you
　　afterward wherever you go,
To gather the minds of men out of their
　　brains as you encounter them, to gather the
　　love out of their hearts,
To take your lovers on the road with you, for
　　all that you leave them behind you,
To know the universe itself as a road, as many
　　roads, as roads for traveling souls.

All parts away for the progress of souls,
All religion, all solid things, arts,
    governments—all that was or is apparent
    upon this globe or any globe, falls into
    niches and corners before the procession
    of souls along the grand roads of the
    universe.

Of the progress of the souls of men and
    women along the grand roads of the
    universe, all other progress is the needed
    emblem and sustenance.

Forever alive, forever forward,
Stately, solemn, sad, withdrawn, baffled, mad,
    turbulent, feeble, dissatisfied,
Desperate, proud, fond, sick, accepted by
    men, rejected by men,
They go! they go! I know that they go, but I
    know not where they go,
But I know that they go toward the best—
    toward something great.
Whoever you are, come forth! or man or
    woman come forth!
You must not stay sleeping and dallying there
    in the house, though you built it, or though
    it has been built for you.

Out of the dark confinement! out from behind
  the screen!
It is useless to protest, I know all and
  expose it.

Behold through you as bad as the rest,
Through the laughter, dancing, dining,
  supping, of people,
Inside of dresses and ornaments, inside
  of those wash'd and trimm'd faces,
Behold a secret silent loathing and despair.

No husband, no wife, no friend, trusted to
  hear the confession,
Another self, a duplicate of every one,
  skulking and hiding it goes,
Formless and wordless through the streets
  of the cities, polite and bland in the
  parlors,
In the cars of railroads, in steamboats, in the
  public assembly,
Home to the houses of men and women,
  at the table, in the bedroom, everywhere,
Smartly attired, countenance smiling, form
  upright, death under the breast-bones, hell
  under the skull-bones,

Under the broadcloth and gloves, under the
    ribbons and artificial flowers,
Keeping fair with the customs, speaking not a
    syllable of itself,
Speaking of any thing else but never of itself.

14

Allons! through struggles and wars!
The goal that was named cannot be
    countermanded.

Have the past struggles succeeded?
What has succeeded? yourself? your nation?
    Nature?
Now understand me well—it is provided in
    the essence of things that from any fruition
    of success, no matter what, shall come
    forth something to make a greater struggle
    necessary.

My call is the call of battle, I nourish active
    rebellion,
He going with me must go well arm'd,
He going with me goes often with spare diet,
    poverty, angry enemies, desertions.

15

Allons! the road is before us!
It is safe—I have tried it—my own feet have
    tried it well—be not detain'd!
Let the paper remain on the desk unwritten,
    and the book on the shelf unopen'd!
Let the tools remain in the workshop! let the
    money remain unearn'd!
Let the school stand! mind not the cry of the
    teacher!
Let the preacher preach in his pulpit! let the
    lawyer plead in the court, and the judge
    expound the law.

Camerado, I give you my hand!
I give you my love more precious than money,
I give you myself before preaching or law;
Will you give me yourself? will you come
    travel with me?
Shall we stick by each other as long as
    we live?